Early Europe

BLOOMSBURY DEBATES IN ARCHAEOLOGY

Series editor: Richard Hodges

Early European Castles

ARISTOCRACY AND AUTHORITY, AD 800-1200

Oliver H. Creighton

B L O O M S B U R Y

LONDON • NEW DELHI • NEW YORK • SYDNEY

Bloomsbury Academic
An imprint of Bloomsbury Publishing Plc

50 Bedford Square	1385 Broadway
London	New York
WC1B 3DP	NY 10018
UK	USA

www.bloomsbury.com

Bloomsbury is a registered trade mark of Bloomsbury Publishing Plc

First published in 2012 by Bristol Classical Press an imprint of
Bloomsbury Academic
Reprinted by Bloomsbury Academic 2013

British Library Cataloguing-in-Publication Data
A catalogue record for this book is available from the British Library.

ISBN: 978-1-7809-3031-2

Library of Congress Cataloging-in-Publication Data
A catalog record for this book is available from the Library of Congress.

Typset by Ray Davies
Printed and bound in Great Britain

Contents

List of Illustrations

List of Illustrations

List of Illustrations

Acknowledgements

Among the host of people who have provided invaluable guidance, information or advice while I was researching this book are: Julia Crick, Lorenz Kemethmüller, Thomas Kühtreiber, Pamela Marshall, Robert Morkot, Keiran O'Conor, Ioana Oltean, Richard Oram and Joachim Zeune. I would like to thank Neil Christie, Suzie Creighton, Michael Fradley, Bob Higham and Duncan Wright for reading and commenting on early drafts of various chapters. Martin Goffriller is also gratefully acknowledged for providing German translations and Mike Rouillard for producing the maps, plans and line-drawings. Daniel Mouton and Jean-Marie Gassend, Terry Barry, Lorenzo Marasco, Kieran O'Conor and Paul Naessens, and Rob Early are thanked for supplying images and are fully acknowledged in the list of illustrations.

The British Academy is also acknowledged for a grant that funded a programme of fieldwork and archival research in support of this and other related publications.

1

Introduction

Studies of medieval castles are not what they used to be. Long perceived, rightly or wrongly, as a stronghold of formidable but sometimes inward-looking scholarship, European castle study or – to use a grander appellation – 'castellology' is being energised by new approaches. Above all, new research is increasingly calling into question the status of the medieval castle as an essentially military artefact, and that is not all: we have the castle as settlement, manor house and estate centre, enmeshed within its landscape; as an icon of lordship; as a literary symbol; and as a domestic arena that reflects its society. Some of these ideas are not novel of course, but reflect existing lines of enquiry given impetus by new research. There is, nonetheless, an undeniable change of emphasis that has grown in forcefulness since the late 1980s: studies of these sites within their broader social, economic and landscape contexts are adding to our established understanding of the multiple military and defensive roles of castles.

But while castle studies are being transformed in many ways, other longstanding trends remain unaltered and unchallenged. One of the more glaringly obvious is that castle scholarship has, with rare exceptions, been pursued within the confines of particular countries and regions. Broader geographical approaches are neglected to the extent that there is only a single scholarly volume on the overall phenomenon of European castles available in English – William Anderson's *Castles of Europe: From Charlemagne to the Renaissance* (1970). A magnificent and weighty exercise in synthesis, this book has nonetheless been overtaken by subsequent archaeological and historical research, and attempts to examine the castle phenomenon on a wider European canvas are conspicuously lacking, despite the strong intellectual rationale for such an approach. After all, were the lords responsible for castle-building not actors within a wider aristocratic culture that shared commonalities of ideology and outlook? Rather than making any claim to offer an alternative pan-European treatment of castle growth and development through the centuries, the essential aim of this book is to show that widening our geographical horizons is a particularly promising way in which castle studies can advance.

Castle studies bring us right to the heart of medieval Europe. These structures were, alongside the great cathedrals, the most recognisable buildings of the Middle Ages. Towering above their settings, they became closely associated with concepts of justice, lordship and authority as well as military might. In some senses, castles came to encapsulate the period's very essence. This introduces a key problem: our knowledge of how castles evolved, and what the 'castle' as an institution came ultimately to represent, colours our understanding of their earliest origins. Too often, we see the genesis of the castle as a point of departure on a line of development – an ever-onward, ever-upward trajectory of increasing technological sophistication towards the *floruit* of European castle architecture in the thirteenth and fourteenth centuries. Such a view is inescapably 'Whig history' – the perception of the past as a march of progress towards an improved present or future. In short, we tend to understand early castles against the background of what they turned into rather than what they were and what they meant in the context of their own contemporary societies and environments.

Too often, studies of medieval European architecture have marginalised castles before *c.* 1200. Frequently caricatured – after the cliché of modernist architecture – as the embodiment of form over function, early castles have often been unfairly portrayed by scholars as robust military installations with forms dictated by defensive pragmatism, lacking the architec-

1. *Introduction*

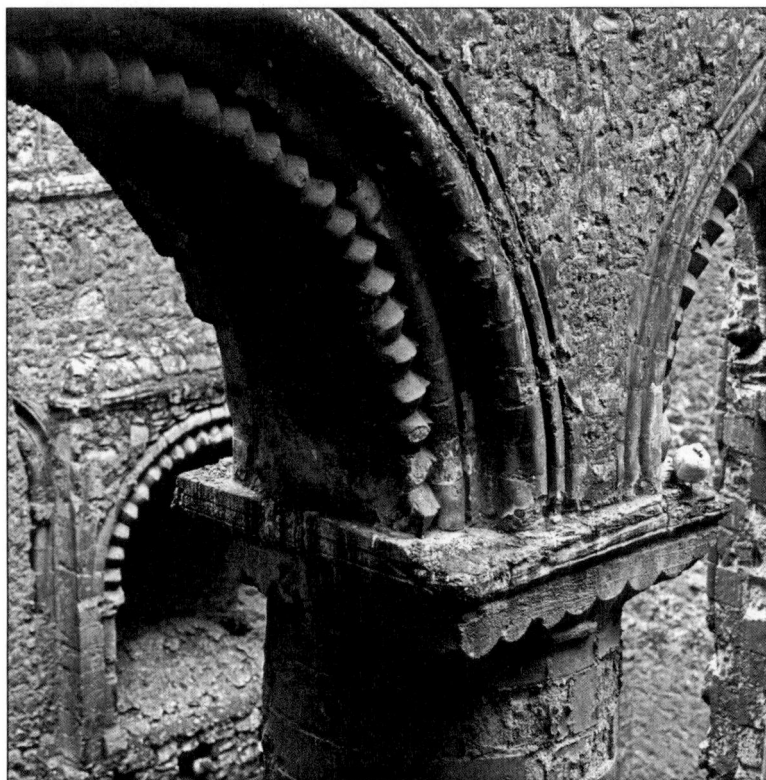

Fig. 1. Romanesque interior of the great tower at Rochester. Constructed for the archbishop of Canterbury in the second quarter of the thirteenth century, the structure incorporates fine architectural sculpture showing the influence of contemporary ecclesiastical architecture on its design.

tural sophistication of contemporary ecclesiastical buildings. Great Romanesque towers in castles certainly borrowed from the same architectural repertoire as contemporary church architecture (Fig. 1), but their perception as grim strongholds is enduring. Even more difficult to shake off is the image of the early castle of earth and timber as simple, humble and altogether inferior to its more glamorous counterpart in stone.

Accordingly, this book sets out a framework for deepening

our understanding of the origins of Europe's earliest castles in the period AD 800-1200, with the aim of providing a platform for fresh debate. The word 'origins' (plural) is important here; it will be shown that there was no single point – either in time or space – from which the castle developed. 'The idol of origins' is a phrase coined by the historian Marc Bloch (1954: 24) to encapsulate the problems inherent in our obsession to search for the earliest development of a phenomenon rather than understand it in its own time and context, and to confuse origins with causes. As we shall see, this is particularly apposite for our understanding of early castles.

Two further distinctive features of the argument developed in this book are worth emphasising from the start. First, it is absolutely essential that the debate about castle origins is not to be driven into a semantic *cul de sac* focused on the origins and meaning of the word 'castle'. Clearly, using historical and archaeological evidence in partnership is of fundamental importance if we are to engage with the subject in a sophisticated way, but we need not start with a debate framed in narrow historical terms. We must also pay full attention to the sheer range of physical evidence for early castles in all its forms – earthworks, architecture and material culture, including the sort of environmental evidence that is too often buried at the back of excavation monographs. Archaeology has a pivotal role to play in uncovering the physical reality of castles to men and women in the early Middle Ages, providing us with a starting point for understanding how people perceived and experienced these buildings, spaces and places. And, as we shall see, fresh archaeological investigations alongside re-appraisals of older work provide us with an ever-enlarging body of evidence, meaning that we must confront some of our preconceptions about the subject based on 'classic' studies of the 1950s and 60s. Secondly, we will look closely at the intimate interrelationship between early castles and the new structures of power and authority that emerged at more or less the same time in Western Europe. In some senses fortification always represented the architecture of power – from Iron Age hillforts to Roman

1. Introduction

military installations and medieval walled cities. A particular
focus in the following discussion is that Europe's earliest castles came to embody a new and radically different form of
power – an aristocratic authority that was highly personal in
nature, glaringly visible in its presence, and enforceable
through violence, both threatened and real.

The following chapter, 'Castle Studies in Transformation',
continues by reflecting critically on some aspects of the historio-
graphy of castle studies – how the subject has developed and
why research has sometimes been constrained by national-
focused approaches – before developing a much-needed rationale for taking seriously the concept of researching
archaeologies of medieval Europe. This establishes the foundations for the third chapter, 'Debating the European Castral
Revolution', which frames the debate over castle origins. The
remainder of the book reviews some of the physical evidence of
early castles at different scales – from towers through to the
spatial planning of castral complexes and their settings – before ending with a conclusion that tentatively proposes some
priorities for future research and seeks to question whether,
indeed, castellology should exist as a discrete subject of research.

2

Castle Studies in Transformation

The term 'castle' means subtly different things to archaeologists, historians and specialists working in other fields. For many, castellology will always be the domain of the architectural historian, with the military backgrounds of many of its early practitioners leaving an indelible mark; for some, it remains a tightly delimited field with its own specialists, methods, terminology, inaccessible literature and academic networks. For newcomers, the very glossary of 'military architecture' can be bewildering. Not only that, but architectural terms have been understood and employed very differently in separate countries, presenting such a huge challenge to work across linguistic boundaries that an entire volume has been dedicated to the comparative terminology of castle studies in the main European languages (Crespi et al. 1975).

There are subtle but important differences even in the basic concept of 'castle' – *Burg* (German), *château* (French), *castello* (Spanish), and *castillo* (Italian) – and its correlation with physical remains on the ground. In French, for example, the word *château* can be applied equally to a country house of the post-medieval period or a fortress of the Middle Ages (although the term *château-fort* has a specifically medieval connotation). In contrast, the German word *Burg* can refer to a miscellany of defended sites, ranging from fortified towns to the earthworks of prehistoric hillforts, meaning that in the German-speaking world debates on castle origins necessarily take on an altogether different meaning. Far from implying the development of seigneurial (or lordly) fortifications as it does in many other parts of Europe, in Germany this process is often taken to

2. Castle Studies in Transformation

mean the re-emergence of hillforts in the fourth and fifth centuries AD – the so-called *Burgenhorizont* or 'castle-building period' – after a long interlude stretching back to the end of the Iron Age (Ettel 2008: 166). Overall, there is little doubt that even in modern scholarship the word 'castle' is used too freely and often uncritically to describe a very wide range of sites.

Castle studies have developed along quite separate lines in different parts of Europe, with distinctive 'schools' of castellology well entrenched, each with their own different priorities, customs and research agendas for the future. Indeed, in some senses the European dimension to the study of castles is actually in retreat. This fact that scholars in different regions and countries have worked within their own research paradigms is a key reason why broader synthesis is so challenging. Furthermore, it is paradoxical that while international fora for the exchange of ideas in European castellology exist, these have tended to perpetuate nationally focused approaches. This is evident in the published proceedings of the biennial *Château Gaillard* colloquium for European castle studies, founded in Caen in 1962. *Château Gaillard* is a European institution but also a barometer of trends in the field over half a century; recent themes for the symposium testify to a gradually widening and increasingly reflective approach, including topics such as 'Castle and settlement' (2004), and 'The perception of the castle' (2010). But while *Château Gaillard* showcases some of the most important scholarship in the field, including dramatic new fieldwork discoveries, contributors to these volumes still overwhelmingly focus on sites within their own discrete regions and countries. This is not so much a criticism, of course, but a reflection of the constricting frameworks within which academic researchers and heritage professionals work.

An important statement on the potential for trans-national approaches to challenge accepted paradigms was made by the ground-breaking cross-channel research of Brian Davison on early forms of timber castles. Through extensive fieldwork in Normandy and comparisons with the English evidence, he was able to demonstrate that mottes were rare here before the mid-eleventh century, with enclosure castles a more typical form of construction (Davison 1969: 39-42). This has important implications for how we have come to understand the role of the Norman Conquest in the origins of castles – as a period of experimentation and innovation rather than involving the transfer of a fully fledged building tradition from one context to another (for further discussion, see p. 62).

French archaeologists and historians have undeniably led the way in early castle research in many respects; for many, the origins of the castle will always belong in France. Formidable academics with towering reputations loomed large over the subject in the twentieth century – figures such as Michel de Boüard, the pioneering excavator of iconic sites such as Caen castle (Normandy), whose plan he recovered from the rubble of Second World War bombings, and Doué-la-Fontaine (Maine-et-Loire), which is still frequently cited as France's or Europe's oldest standing castle. Equally influential is the contribution of French medieval historians such as Georges Duby and Marc Bloch, whose research has done so much to illuminate the social and economic milieu in which early castles flourished. Nonetheless, the enduring tradition in France of region-specific programmes of fieldwork and excavation and monographs dealing with particular geographical areas means that the overall picture of early castle growth can appear fragmented from an archaeological point of view. Castle studies have not always enjoyed a centre stage position in medieval scholarship elsewhere in Europe. In the Netherlands, for example, academic study of castles always occupied a rather peripheral position, carrying something of a stigma until quite recently. Nonetheless, there are signs that this will change if interdisciplinary approaches are adopted in which the understanding of the place of fortification within the entire medieval settlement pattern is seen as central to the research agenda (Janssen 2008: 247-8).

Within the context of these very varied traditions of research around Europe, the movement towards broader social and economic interpretations of castles nevertheless emerges as a consistent theme in the late twentieth and early twenty-first centuries. In parts of Europe such as Italy and Ireland, castellology is quite fully integrated into rural settlement history and lordly fortifications feature prominently in narratives of the making of the medieval countryside, as Chapter 7 explores in more detail. The work of Swiss archaeologists has also been influential in changing perspectives about the social and economic roles of castles, with Werner Meyer's excavations at Alt-Wartburg in the canton of Aargau in the late 1960s especially important in investigating outlying sectors of this fortification, including an associated economic zone that dated, like the first castle, to the late twelfth century (Zeune 1996: 35). Since the 1980s, Swedish castellology has in some senses led the way in developing contextual approaches, with the hinterland emphasis developing early so that projects developed at Faxholm, in Hälsingland, and Krapperup, in north-west Scania, could use the castle as a point of departure for understanding issues of land-use, economy and settlement rather than a discrete focus of enquiry in its own right (Mogren 1996). In Germany, site-specific and often architecturally focused approaches have tended to hold sway, furnishing us with numerous superbly detailed case studies of castle construction and evolution, but with landscape approaches underdeveloped.

Nationalism has played a key role in the development of castellology, and national research agendas continue to frame the construction of knowledge. An extreme example of how early castle research has furthered nationalist agendas is the career of the influential German architectural historian, restorer and founder of the German Castle Society, Bodo Ebhardt, in the early twentieth century. He saw the first castles as *völkisch* (folk/ethnic) symbols and argued not only for the Germanic origin of castles in Europe but also the medieval social order itself; tellingly, Nazi politicians in the 1930s seized upon such ideas to justify German territorial expansion (Link 2009: 327). Francoist Spain furnishes us with other revealing examples of early castle heritage manipulated to fit nationalist narratives. The development of the Alcázar in Toledo, a site

19

that originated as a Roman palace and was later reused as a royal castle, as a 'patriotic' tourist destination is a case in point. Franco's rebuilding and presentation of this prominent hilltop fortress celebrated an iconic Republican defeat here in 1936 and referenced more distant martial distant heritage including Alfonso VI's capture of the site from the Muslims in 1085 (Basilio 2004).

While the state has sometimes glorified early castles as cultural markers of national identity, in other contexts research has avoided or marginalised them and the contentious heritage they can represent. In the Republic of Ireland, for example, we can attribute the marked lack of attention that early castles received through much of the twentieth century to their enduring association in the minds of many with Norman colonial oppression and English rule. Only relatively recently have the numerous mottes and masonry castles of the Norman period been accepted in any sense as 'national' monuments, and in the early part of the twenty-first century castle studies in Ireland show every sign of flourishing, with important and energetic new surveys and excavation led by the Discovery Programme shedding new light on fortifications built for Gaelic dynasts as well as Anglo-Norman lords (Barry 2008). By way of contrast, archaeologists in Northern Ireland carried out several seminal excavations of early earth and timber castles as far back as the 1950s and 60s, including the important investigations of mottes at Rathmullan and Castleskreen in County Down, revealing that Norman lords superimposed these fortifications upon native Irish sites.

Medieval archaeologies of Europe?

Medieval archaeology *in* Europe and the archaeology *of* medieval Europe are quite different things. A central argument of this book is that medieval archaeology urgently needs more supra-national archaeological research, taking into account developments across large geographical areas as well as comparative work between different regions and countries. A broader-based approach to castle studies is one example of how we might move towards this goal.

The case for attempting to research and write 'medieval archaeologies of Europe' might seem so obvious as to be unworthy of detailed argument. There clearly existed a medieval concept of Europe closely linked to the very notion of Christendom; surely we cannot hope to understand the medieval archaeologies of modern nations in isolation from one another? Surely research engaging with big questions across wide geographical areas is desirable for the health and profile of medieval archaeology?

That said, we should not treat the need to pursue broader geographical approaches uncritically. Trans-national studies must confront obvious practical challenges, but there are philosophical ones too. The definition and concept of medieval Europe as a discrete entity worthy of study in its own right, forming a natural and logical scale of enquiry, is not without its problems. The very notion of a European past brings with it considerable cultural and ideological baggage and the concept is inextricably entwined with the issue of European integration in the twenty-first century. It is vital, of course, that any aspiration towards trans-national research should be more than the product of modern political agendas, in particular 'Europeanisation' and the furtherance of a collective EU identity. There also exists a more insidious danger that singling out Europe as a natural focus of enquiry can embody cultural superiority, explicitly or implicitly. Such an approach could elevate Europe (or perhaps more specifically Western Europe) as being somehow more central, important or influential than others in the Middle Ages, serving to sever it from the other geographical zones with which it interacted, most notably the Islamic and Eastern European spheres.

Equally, recognition of some sort of underlying common European medieval heritage should not deny the diversity of past cultures and landscapes within its ambit, nor impose models based on a supposed European core to regions where they do not work and are neither valid nor welcome. A particularly clear example of precisely this is the widespread tendency to understand medieval structures of lordship and authority in relation to the Anglo-French experience, where a so-called 'feudal' model supposedly operated – a notion that is deconstructed in the following chapter.

So, do we really need archaeologies of Europe? To the Danish prehistorian Kristian Kristiansen (2008), writing on this question, the answer is, emphatically, 'yes'; European archaeology *sans frontières* must be our ultimate goal. But moving towards this ambition is proving increasingly difficult in the face of challenges inextricably linked to post-modern fashions within the subject, especially the post-processual emphasis on the immediate contexts within which individuals lived their lives and experienced past worlds. There has arguably been a fundamental shift in the scale of archaeological enquiry generally since the 1980s: the growth of the local, regional and national perspectives has seen European approaches in full retreat. Monolingualism remains another obvious hurdle, with an alarming decline in reading and citing other languages in archaeological publication, while teaching and textbooks are arguably weighted increasingly towards national perspectives (Kristiansen 2008: 14-22). In parts of Central and Eastern Europe, meanwhile, nationally focused approaches to medieval archaeology are closely linked to the bolstering of social and political identities in the post-Communist world.

But this debate over the growth of the 'national paradigm' in archaeological research largely concerns prehistory. And therein is a paradox. The tendency to favour national and local perspectives is arguably more acute still within medieval archaeology – the very branch of the subject for which the pan-European approach arguably holds greatest potential. Prehistory has a background of supra-national research aims, with established master-works of synthesis of the sort that medieval archaeology has largely lacked. Incredibly, only in the early years of the twenty-first century has European medieval archaeology produced a first textbook/synthesis accessible to undergraduate students (Graham-Campbell with Valor 2007).

2. Castle Studies in Transformation

In contrast, the sweeping European synthesis has long been central to medieval history (see, for example, Bartlett 1993; Wickham 2005). The irony, of course, is that for later medieval archaeologists 'Europe' is not an abstract concept at all; it is far more than a modern political construct or a convenient geographical container. The very essence of Europe was arguably rooted in the Middle Ages: it was both an idea and a geographical entity that was meaningful to contemporaries of the period (Le Goff 2005).

The lack of broader perspectives is especially acute within later medieval archaeology (taken here to cover the twelfth to fifteenth centuries). To early medievalists engaging with great themes such as the migration period or the Viking diaspora, the European dimension to study has perhaps come more naturally. In contrast, most archaeologists of the later medieval period work exclusively within individual countries. A further issue here is the trend towards compartmentalisation within the subject, meaning its division into discrete and sometimes cosy areas of scholarship – the 'sub-sets' of medieval archaeology, of which castellology is of course one, alongside rural settlement studies, monastic archaeology, artefact studies and so on. What makes the European approach particularly apposite for the study of castle origins is that the social elite that built and lived in these structures demonstrably had a supranational outlook. A pivotal question is the role of the castle in the process of 'Europeanisation' and the increasing homogenisation of culture up to c. 1300, as manifested in aspects of life as diverse as patterns or naming, the growth of university educations, the popularity of saints' cults and the usage of coinage (Bartlett 1993: 269-91). Networks of elite cultural contact and patronage spanned modern state boundaries, and patterns of land-holding sometimes did likewise. The well attested 'aristocratic diaspora' of the tenth to thirteenth centuries that saw colonisation, conquest and adventuring on a huge scale is another reason why trans-national approaches are the only sophisticated way of engaging with archaeologies of the medieval elite.

Pursuing medieval archaeologies of Europe clearly brings with it enormous challenges. The subject has expanded dramatically in the last half-century and our data set has exploded accordingly. When many working in local and regional contexts are struggling under the sheer weight of newly available information, where does this leave our ambition to broaden geographical horizons still further? Others might question the relevance of Europeanism to practitioners working for heritage agencies and in commercial units necessarily engaged at local and regional levels. One riposte is that it is only through widened understandings across broader geographical areas that we can truly appreciate the distinctiveness of more localised cultures – whether or not they were typical of the wider scene. Another is that medieval archaeology quite simply needs to be less provincial; its internationalisation should be a sign of maturity and confidence, ensuring a heighted profile and creating the potential for greater recognition within and impact upon other disciplines.

Summary

With few exceptions castellology has traditionally abstained from trans-national approaches, which is unfortunate given the rich potential for study across a wider European canvas. Despite complex conceptual and philosophical as well as obvious practical challenges, this mode of study can widen research horizons and is essential if we are to engage in any meaningful way with the construction of elite identities in the early Middle Ages.

3

Debating the European Castral Revolution

Castles were, of course, not the only fortifications active in Europe in the period AD 800-1200. The ninth and tenth centuries in particular saw a high level of innovation and experimentation with different forms of defence-work, of which the castle was only one manifestation. At the same time, fortifications belonging to long-established traditions remained in use and received continuing investment, most obviously walled towns. We can make a useful distinction here between 'communal fortifications' that protected civilian populations in periods of tension and 'early state fortifications' that were built to defend borders or other militarily sensitive areas (De Meulemeester and O'Conor 2007: 316-23).

Aside from the fortified urban settlement, another important tradition of communal defence was the hill-top fortress (although coastal equivalents are also known), either newly planned or a re-activation of an Iron Age or Roman site. Many accommodated threatened populations only periodically, and archaeologically their interiors are sometimes blank. The term 'state fortifications' embraces a miscellany of guard posts, garrisoned fortresses and fortified bridges and extends to include linear fortifications such as the Danevirke in Denmark, whose complex evolution between the eighth and eleventh centuries reflects the changing nature of military leadership in the region. Traditional explanations of the castle-building phenomenon have sought to draw a sharp distinction between these types of fortification, which are all in some way 'public' in the sense that they protected populations, and the 'private' nature of the castle.

Defining the castle: the eternal question

It is impossible to get much further without coming up against problems of definition: what is a castle? This is a notoriously difficult and contentious area. Moreover, there is a danger that the amount of scholarly attention devoted to attempting to answer this ultimately unanswerable question can deflect our attention away from the more fundamental concerns of what these sites looked like and what they meant to contemporaries. Most important of all, we should be aware of the problems of fitting cultural artefacts of the medieval world into modern definitions. There can be no precise criteria for what castles were; medieval society's own understanding of what the word meant developed through time, while individuals from different backgrounds understood castles very differently.

From one point of view, the sites covered in this book might seem a heterogeneous bunch, ranging from earth and timber strongholds to monumental edifices of stone. Indeed, we might legitimately question whether in a hypothetical prehistoric scenario – if we were stripped of our preconceptions and knowledge of the medieval world based on historical sources – we would put such sites in the same category. Consequently, the approach taken here is that we should define the early castle as much by its social context as its physical appearance, the technologies used in its construction, or the character and seriousness of its defences. Seigneurial (or lordly) residences appeared over Europe in very varied forms, and the distinction between these and castles is not at all clear cut. In the succinct words of De Meulemeester and O'Conor: 'castles were, in some way, fortified private homes ...', but '... not all defended private residences were castles' (2007: 324).

The functions that modern scholars have ascribed to castles are many, varied and in some cases apparently contradictory. Nonetheless, it is useful at this stage to think briefly and very generally about their essential attributes: what they looked like physically; what went on in and around them; and who built and lived within them. These matters might seem sufficiently obvious as to not warrant repeating, but it is worth reflecting once again how scholarship has tended to break the early castle-building phenomenon down into different developments in different regions and to classify and sub-classify sites into different types. It is instructive, however, to pull back from this detail and identify some underlying commonalities in the functions, appearances and spatial ordering of sites.

All early castles were, of course, in some contexts defensive installations and strong points from which the surrounding countryside could be harassed and intimidated. But they were also homes, hunting seats and places for leisurely living as well as farms and the hubs of estates. In a less concrete but critically important way they were symbols of power projection. Finally, the castle provided a staged setting where lord, household and the wider community played out rituals old and new, including meetings of the court, the collection of taxes, and 'homage' ceremonies that marked the legal bonds between lord and tenant.

In terms of its physical appearance to a medieval onlooker, the essential defining quality of the early castle was that it was generally tall and small (Fig. 2). They were physically elevated yet compact, certainly in comparison to the areas covered by walled towns and other communal fortifications, and this characteristic is as true of sites built in earth and timber as those realised in stone. Whatever the technology of its construction, the outward appearance of an early castle was also usually rounded, curved or irregular, while the buildings and structures within it, whether for meeting, sleeping and resting, worship, storage or agricultural production, were virtually without exception rectangular, with the combination of *camera-aula-capella* (chamber, hall and chapel) usually core to the domestic plan. This contrast is important: while defences would have been remarkable and unusual and hid the interior from view, the domestic quarters within the enceinte adhered to fundamental rules of organisation common across the medieval world, signalling the operation of traditional hierarchies behind the façade. What differs is their scale and complexity,

27

Fig. 2. Reconstruction of Niozelles, showing a small late tenth-century castle in Provence.

depending largely upon the status and wealth of their occupants. The essential spatial grammar of planning was consistent.

Another unifying characteristic of the spatial organisation of the early castle was its subdivision into two or more subsidiary units, invariably with a tower or some other building as its focal point. To this were appended one or more additional units – often styled as baileys (from the Latin *ballium*) or wards, although the German distinction between *Hauptburg* (principal unit) and *Vorburg* (outer enclosed zone) is also helpful. The activities contained within varied immensely, but often included domestic facilities, agricultural functions, industry and settlement; what is consistent is that these spaces were always tangibly of higher or lower status relative to one another in terms of their buildings, functions and the people who lived and circulated in and around them.

Finally, confusion can also arise because of the diverse nature of castle-building society. This actually comprised a broad social group that what we might loosely define as the medieval 'elite': from emperors, kings, dukes, counts, viscounts and bishops, down to relatively petty lords whose influence was felt only at a local level. The castle was not something that we can define easily and unambiguously; rather, the castle 'idea' was a remarkably flexible template, adaptable to a huge variety of different tenurial, social and geographical circumstances.

Castles and the 'new aristocracy'

A central concern of this book is the intimate relationship between early castles and new structures of power and authority. The classic story is that the splintering of the Carolingian Empire – at its peak covering some one million square kilometres of Europe – in the ninth and tenth centuries saw hard-pressed rulers delegate authority, with counts and viscounts tasking control of *pagi* (or counties), which were themselves sub-divided as private lords carved out a multitude of private domains (castellanies or castelries) amidst a growing vacuum of centralised control. Aristocrats fortified their estate centres, driven by security needs but by also social competition as they endeavoured to ape their rulers and rival or surpass their peers. The key ingredients of this aristocratic identity were the conspicuous display of power and martial prowess – what the medieval historian Robert Bartlett has termed the 'self image of the conqueror' (1993: 85). Such are the commonalities of outlook within Europe's new aristocracy that it might be valid to think about these social groups sharing a common worldview and their residences a 'spatial ideology' (Hansson 2006). How was this aristocratic image constructed and how and why did it manifest itself through castle building?

In the context of the longer-term development of aristocratic identity across Western Europe, the castle was but one manifestation of a trend whereby individuals marked their status through permanent buildings rather than personal effects and portable exotica, which were the forms of display characterising the more mobile elites of the immediately preceding period (Costambeys et al. 2011: 286). Also integral to this new ideology was the active cultivation of a sense of social separateness and distinction. Aristocratic identity was rooted in cultural and intellectual superiority as manifested in aspects of behaviour such as language and personal appearance as well as participation in socially restricted activities including hunting. Important too was the demonstration to wider populations of noble legitimacy based on family lineage – a subject that has been hotly debated by medieval historians who have long disagreed on the importance of a social 'mutation' around AD 1000 and whether or not this was fundamental to the triumph of lineage characterised by primogeniture (Crouch 2005: 99-123). Finally, we should not overlook the simple fact that this was an elite whose power was rooted in the countryside, and it is unsurprisingly in the rural sphere rather than in established towns and cities that we see prodigious early castle building. Indeed, we might question whether this was a conscious and quite deliberate means through which the new aristocracy created an identity removed from ancient urban power bases associated with church and state.

Castles became indispensible elements within this emerging vocabulary of lordship, the ordering of their structures and settings used actively to create, perpetuate and reinforce a culture of nobility. Crucially, all the key aspects of noble identity coalesced in the idea of the castle. Put simply: a castle was a symbol of wealth, because only individuals with access to privileges and resources could build one; and a display of martial prowess through its outwardly and recognisably military appearance, embodying the new social role of violence. A castle was also a symbol of social distinction in more subtle ways than its elevated appearance: its architecture proclaimed the social connections of its owner and their participation in elite knowledge networks. As an ancestral seat, each castle symbolised the heritage and legitimacy of the family in question as well as their need to have stable centres of estate administration. Castles were 'title deeds in stone' and monuments dedicated to

3. Debating the European Castral Revolution

Fig. 3. *Belli Locus*: the monastery founded by Fulk Nerra, Count of Anjou, within sight of his castle at Loches.

the memories of noble families – a connection which became all the more powerful when the fortress was twinned (as was so often the case) with a religious institution that doubled as a dynastic mausoleum (Fig. 3). At another level, however, the materialisation of these private lordships was indicative of a new *mentalité* – an aristocratic mindset prepared to bring order to the landscape with the castle and the castral district at its heart.

Political undertones are never far away from how we interpret the social roles and contexts of these early castles. To some the early European nobility might appear as brave young capitalists: entrepreneurial generators of individual wealth they could hand to the next generation, aggressively taking advantage of a flabby and moribund state and privatising not only the means of defence, but also the operation of justice. For others, however, the origins of castles embody class conflict. To the French medieval historian Marc Bloch, one of the founders of the *Annales* School of history, castles 'cast a perpetual shadow over the fields of Europe; they provided the essential apparatus for lords to 'defend themselves and dominate others' (Bloch 1961: 300-1).

Early castles: multiple origins

We can interpret 'the origins of castles' in multiple ways. First, we must differentiate the overall phenomenon of castle building from the origins of individual sites, and we cannot even vaguely hope to understand the former without detailed reference to the latter. It is crucial to note here, therefore, that a distinct point of origin for any given castle can sometimes be hard to distinguish in the material evidence, not least because their earliest phases are so difficult to come to grips with archaeologically. Excavation of early castles in different parts of Europe has often revealed long-term sequences of high-status occupation on sites whose appearances and defences evolved gradually through time, in many cases over several centuries. In such a sequence, the point at which a castle existed as opposed to some other supposed category of lordly site or fortification becomes a matter of interpretation.

Overall, the castle origins debate has probably suffered from excessive focus on developments in France, England and (to a lesser extent) Germany. Castle building also clearly took place at very different paces in different places and in certain parts of Europe lordly fortifications were exceptionally few or late-comers to the landscape, as in many parts of Scandinavia. Norway, for example, has a very sparse distribution of castles – including a couple of examples north of the Arctic Circle – as royal power retarded their development and the noble classes were less fixed; the absence of castles fed into early nationalist narratives that portrayed a medieval landscape of farmers free from feudal oppression (Ekroll 1998: 65). Castles in Finland were late and principally related to Swedish conquests from the thirteenth century onwards, and although noble families played a greater role in castle building in Denmark and Sweden, examples before the thirteenth century are rare indeed and it was the fourteenth century that witnessed the real explosion of private castle building (Liebgott and Olsen 2008). These developments are still an important part of the castle origins narrative, however, as they still had impacts on local landscapes and societies that were in their own contexts, every bit as profound as apparently more prodigious events elsewhere. For example, in the medieval landscape of Småland, on the border between Sweden and Denmark, private castles were unknown before the late thirteenth and early fourteenth centuries, after which members of the minor gentry classes made their mark by constructing them in characteristically visible locations – especially islands and peninsulas – rather than in places with maximum agricultural potential, in order to evoke a castle-like image (Hansson 2001). Within their own environments such seigneurial sites represented a visibly new and even revolutionary presence rather than something derivative.

A particularly important consideration is the bewildering array of words used in Latin charters and chronicles to describe sites that may or may not equate to castles. It is important to remember that early medieval writers clearly applied the terms *castrum* and *castellum* quite widely to embrace walled towns, palaces and even monastic sites, as well as castles and sometimes their territories. All such references have to be interpreted in their correct context. In Ireland before the Norman conquest of 1169, for instance, native chroniclers used derivative terms such as *caislén* and *caistél* to describe fortifications built by powerful Gaelic lords in early twelfth-century Connaught, giving rise to a lively debate over whether they constitute castles, either as perceived by medieval contemporaries or as defined by present-day archaeologists (O'Conor et al. 2010: 34). Clearly used to label installations that were somehow new and different, in this context an interpretation that native builders were drawing on a long-established tradition of fortification but building on an increasing scale rather than buying into the European mainstream seems preferable (see pp. 104-7).

Across large swathes of western and southern Europe, documentary evidence apparently testifies to the multiplication and rapid spread of castles after the magic year AD 1000: in Pierre Toubert's classic study (1973) of the Lazio region they sprang up like mushrooms in the night, tripling and even quadrupling every half century as testified in charter evidence. To take as an example a different region that has been the subject of painstaking research: in the dramatic, mountainous area of the Vivrais in south-east France, between the Rhone Valley and the Massif Central, the first castles appeared in the period 970-80, with around 76 in existence by *c.* 1100 and 153 by the close of the thirteenth century (Laffont 2009). The challenges of mapping these sites are considerable, however.

In some cases the likelihood is that medieval writers were using essentially generic terms, as in the aforementioned case of *castrum* and *castellum*, but also *firmitas* (strongpoint), *forcia* (fortification) and *munitio* (defence-work), while *oppidum* (city) was also occasionally employed. More rarely, specific words potentially give insight into aspects of construction and appearance. These include: *agger* (earthwork, in some cases perhaps implying a mound or motte); *vallum* (a bank or rampart, perhaps in some cases a palisade); and *turris* (tower) or *dungio* (donjon or great tower), although the latter could be of stone or wood and in certain contexts these words equated to a 'stronghold' more generally.

Attempts to correlate such references with specific types of physical structure and to use this evidence to map the spread of the castle phenomenon are hazardous indeed, and need always to be informed by painstaking analysis of the primary source material and a consideration of the author's biases, knowledge and the reliability of their terminology. There is sometimes little consistency in individual sources, let alone between writers in different parts of Europe, who of course suited their choice of word to the specific context of the prose in question. A key issue here, therefore, is the contrast between the rather sudden appearance and spread of 'castles' in the documentary record and the growing body of archaeological evidence testifying long-term sequences of aristocratic occupation on individual sites, as alluded to above. There are good reasons to pause and consider whether the apparent explosion of castle building was a *révélation documentaire* rather than reflecting what was really happening on the ground.

We should also remember that the 'origin' of a given site as understood by an archaeologist and as appreciated by a medieval contemporary might be very different things indeed. To take as one famous example: London's famous White Tower. To the archaeologist, the site's origins might now seem relatively secure, attributable in no small way to a recent programme of structural survey and documentary analysis that forms a model of integrated analysis (Impey 2008). The various strands of dating evidence agree: we can confidently attribute the structure to around 1075-9; William I ordered its construction within an earlier Norman power-base of earth and timber built in 1066-7, itself occupying one corner of the ancient Roman city walls. Yet inhabitants of medieval London would have seen the origins of the site very differently. Foundation myths current in the Middle Ages variously attributed the White Tower to the ancient British King Belinus and to Julius Caesar, and it was associated in the minds of many with the legends of King Arthur (Wheatley 2008: 65-74). Whether such mythologies were cultivated purposefully remains a subject for debate; we can be certain, however, that they created a sense of deep antiquity, conveying the impression that the mighty tower was far older than it really was.

Debates over castle origins are delicate, as it is not long before we have to confront long-treasured beliefs and ideas; and they are complex, because these developments took place over great tracts of territory. Moreover, the strands of evidence are all problematic in some way; using them in combination holds greater challenges still. We are confronted with a meagre collection of standing buildings and the earthworks of field monuments prone to destruction and re-use; a smattering of excavations, often with imperfect dating evidence, whose results are prone to re-interpretation; and a sparse assortment of documents, often maddeningly inconsistent in their terminology. Nonetheless, a dramatic growth in available archaeological data, allied to fresh theoretical approaches, can open up different perspectives on the European 'castral revolution'.

Confronting the narrative of castle origins

Traditional models for understanding and explaining the origins of the castle-building phenomenon have rested on three basic tenets. First, scholarship has continued to see early castle growth as inextricably linked to the development of a new type of social organisation known as feudalism. Second, the phenomenon of castle building is rooted in France, whence it diffused outwards across Europe. Third, early castles represent an entirely new species of fortification in terms of their 'private' status, something inherently different from the 'public' forms of defence that characterised preceding periods. The following section introduces and briefly discusses these pillars of the 'origins of the castle' debate as essential context for the subsequent chapters, which turn to the physical realities of structures and their landscapes.

Re-thinking the feudal castle

What then ... is the evidence for castles, for private as opposed to public fortifications, for the fortified residence of a lord, in pre-Conquest England? Answer, there is none (Allen Brown 1969: 140).

To R. Allen Brown in his archaeologist-baiting paper 'An historian's approach to the origins of the castle in England' it was self-evident that because late Anglo-Saxon England was not a 'feudal' society, there could not have been any castles. The message was clear: castles and feudalism (and more specifically 'feudal society') go together, as it were, hand in glove. For generations of scholars feudalism formed the essential explanatory framework for understanding the genesis of the castle; put simply, the feudal revolution emanating from France around AD 1000 was axiomatic with the growth of private defence.

3. Debating the European Castral Revolution

There are now good reasons to question whether we should continue to view the rise of the castle through the prism of a feudal narrative. Feudalism has become a dirty word for many historians; revisionism has blown apart the notion of it as an homogeneous system providing the glue that held medieval society together in its famous pyramid. Castle-builders in no way saw themselves as feudal; the concept is not authentically medieval but a legal construct of the sixteenth and seventeenth centuries. In a radically revisionist study Susan Reynolds (1994) exposed the medieval feudal system as a vacuous concept; one of its supposedly most characteristic features, vassalage (meaning relationships between lords and dependants), did not emerge out of early medieval warrior societies but was rooted in the bureaucracy of estate administration in the twelfth and thirteenth centuries. Other medieval historians have seized upon the blurred distinction between land that was 'held' and 'owned' to dismantle the very concept of feudalism; in the eleventh century nobles and even peasants in different parts of Europe held 'allodial' rights to property (meaning full rights to their land). It should be emphasised that it is primarily the idea of a feudal 'system' that has been assaulted; feudal as an adjective from *feudum* (fief or fee) remains a useful part of historians' vocabularies.

It is quite clear that private fortifications existed in very diverse social environments around early medieval Europe and not only in supposedly feudalised contexts. Early medieval Spain provides us with an instructive contrast between the different social roles of castles in areas under Christian and Islamic control in the tenth and eleventh centuries. In Christian Catalonia castles were clearly central to what has been termed the 'feudalisation' of a society where bonds of dependence were strong, while in Al-Andalus Muslim lords built equivalent castle-like fortifications within the context of a tribal framework and a strongly kin-based society (Glick 2005: 250-44). The notion of the castle at the heart of a 'feudal' landscape is similarly invalid in Denmark, the Nordic countries and the Slavonic principalities around the Baltic, which

37

never developed in any sense as feudal states. Fresh research directions taking account of these very varied experiences are now opening up new landscapes of debate about feudalism (Bagge et al. 2011).

Another danger inherent in the model of the 'feudal castle' is that it can encourage a top-down view of the medieval world dominated by research into the medieval elite. No matter how broadly defined, this social group represented a tiny sub-set within medieval society, and a central concern of a mature approach to early castles must be how these sites interfaced with wider populations. Archaeologies of castles need not always equate to the material culture of the social elite; investigation of these sites can tell us about trade networks, agricultural management and settlement development, for example.

While feudalism is in a strict sense quite a narrow concept, the early castle was the product of more deeply rooted changes to the structure, makeup and outlook of Europe's aristocracy. These saw families tie themselves to particular localities – a stability augmented by new patrilineal systems of inheritance (i.e. ancestral descent through the male line) that meant fewer heirs and an altogether more streamlined aristocracy (Airlie 1995: 436-7). The castle was the supreme physical manifestation of noble culture and a product of these social changes; it may have been the 'instrument of a [feudal] revolution' (Bur 1982), but, crucially, it was not its root cause.

This latter point brings to mind the famous but now heavily discredited 'stirrup thesis' proposed by the historian of medieval technology Lynn White Jr in his book *Military Technology and Social Change* (1963: 1-38). In essence, this singled out the stirrup's introduction into the Carolingian world from Asia as the key causal factor behind the growth of feudalism. Allowing lance-armed cavalry to rule supreme on the battlefield because it allowed a mounted man to remain on his horse despite the impact of a charge, it ultimately explained the rise of the knightly classes and the system of landholding that sustained them. It is ironic that while White's thesis was soon met with

vigorous and sustained criticism on the grounds of his perceived technological determinism (the belief that technology
drives social change) (Roland 2003), it was more than thirty
years later that the very notion of feudalism itself was cri-
tiqued and deconstructed. What are the implications of this for
the debate around early castle growth? First, it would be wrong
to substitute 'castle' for 'stirrup' and see early fortifications as
the result of a technological breakthrough that had a series of
knock-on effects on society. This was manifestly not the case,
as all the technologies employed in their construction were
current and well established, as covered in more detail in the
following two chapters. Second, it is too easy to classify early
private fortifications as 'feudal castles'; indeed, archaeologists
should probably stop using the word 'feudal' altogether. We
package many things together when we use the word, when its
meaning is actually tightly circumscribed.

All this leaves us in a somewhat awkward position: the
'feudal revolution' never happened but the 'castle revolution'
did. We might reconcile this position by taking a more open
view that sees the castle not as a monolithic institution but as
a remarkably flexible model and an idea rooted in a new aristocratic ideology.

Questioning diffusionism

European medieval history is essentially French history;
everything starts in France, from administration, architecture and Arthurian romances, through chivalry,
crusades and castles, to universities and water-mills
(Reuter 1997: 187-8).

These satirical remarks remind us that the notion of castles
diffusing across Europe, from a seminal locus in northern
France to the continent's peripheries, is not only ingrained
deeply within castle scholarship, but within medieval studies
more generally. Traditional lines of enquiry have sought to
identify likely points of origin in the form of buildings that

broke the mould; to locate early centres of castle building; and to search for the axes of communication along which these ideas were transmitted. Archaeologists and historians alike traditionally portray France as the centre of early castle development, with the area around the Loire valley witnessing particularly early and significant events. Experience tells us that we should be wary, however, of big bold models whereby a 'new' style of monument diffuses neatly over large tracts of territory. For example, a note of caution is sounded by recent deconstruction of the Romanesque architectural style as a pan-European phenomenon; despite superficial unity, it can alternatively be seen as a complex and interwoven 'quilt' of local styles and regional developments (O'Keeffe 2007). It is important to understand why castles developed early on in some regions, and it is also instructive to consider why their arrival in others was more sluggish, as these developments are still part of a 'castle origins' debate.

From France, the traditional model sees early castle growth spread (through acculturation) across the Rhine westwards into Germany and (through conquest) to England, then Ireland, Scotland and Wales. In some of these contexts the origins of castles have been closely tied to the arrival of incoming groups – what we might term the 'ethnic origin of castles' thesis. We should certainly remember that architecture did not diffuse on its own accord, somehow influencing the forms of other structures. Architectural historians sometimes fit buildings into complex 'family trees' in which structures are interrelated with one another through supposed lineage. We must remember that the agency of individuals – in particular the dynamic between builders and patrons, and the knowledge networks they were part of – is crucial to explaining how architectural forms were chosen and adapted. The classic 'origins of the castle' model is actually very specific to quite limited zones of Western Europe. Diverse regions of central and eastern Europe witnessed the emergence of broadly comparable aristocratic societies associated with their own traditions of defence that bear comparison with castles, although they are often labelled in different ways.

3. Debating the European Castral Revolution

Scholars have developed very different narratives for the emergence of castles in different parts of Europe. In England, a famously acrimonious debate focused on whether there is archaeological or historical evidence for Anglo-Saxon private defended residences – especially those of 'thegns' (lesser nobles) – that equated in a functional sense to castles before 1066 (Williams 2008: 85-104). One of the most important contexts for the castle origins debate is in Ireland, meanwhile, where archaeological investigation is showing that power-holders within early medieval Gaelic societies built precursors to castles, as in the Shannon region, where chiefs built fortified sites, sometimes in stone, before the Anglo-Norman colonisation. But elsewhere debates are less focused on castles as they might be understood in Britain, Ireland or France. In Italy the emergence of castles cannot be severed from a wider debate about *incastellamento*, meaning the nucleation of communities on hilltop sites. In Spain, a very different debate contrasts Muslim fortifications of the period with the first Christian castles in the tenth century, and the entire narrative is tied up to the contentious clash between these civilisations. In Germany the late tenth and early eleventh centuries saw strong royal government in the form of the Ottonian dynasty and sprawling palaces rather than compact castles remaining the predominant tradition, so that debates over new forms of fortification must be related to the emergence of a strong state. In large areas of central Europe including parts of modern-day Austria, the Czech Republic and Poland, an important archaeological debate concerns the functions of early medieval hilltop strongholds of the ninth and tenth centuries containing evidence of industry and the presence of elite families. While elsewhere in Europe these sites might equate in some way to proto-castles, in this context attention focuses on whether or not they were urban in nature.

What is clear is that a broader geographical approach to the question of castle origins is needed that extends the discussion beyond the supposed cradle of early private fortification in northern France, taking in sites and landscapes distributed more widely across the continent. Castles did not originate as the result of some technological achievement or breakthrough – an experimental structure such as the donjon formed by heightening a hall at Doué-la-Fontaine was not a 'Eureka moment' (see pp. 66-8). The European landscape was already studded with the towers of ecclesiastical buildings by the time of the first waves of castle building; the innovation was translating the idea to the private seigneurial sphere. Crucially, there was no point of castle 'origin' as such – rather a suite of different beginnings in different contexts across a span of time that in all likelihood extended over several centuries.

Challenging the military paradigm

A long-established historical narrative has established that in the eighth and ninth centuries AD three external threats – from Saracens, Magyars and Vikings – saw marauding armies penetrate deep into the heart of early medieval Europe, creating a challenging military landscape dotted with increasing densities of fortifications. Internal struggles between rival claimants to the heritage of the Carolingian Empire exacerbated insecurity in this period, which forms an essential context for the genesis of the castle. From the south, the Saracens threatened France and then Italy in the eighth and ninth centuries; by the tenth and eleventh centuries they also erected powerful fortifications of their own in the form of *alcazabas*. These were hilltop strongholds or citadels, usually comprising turreted enceintes of *tapía* or rammed earth, such as the immense examples on the southern coast of Spain at Málaga and Almería (Fig. 4), which rulers built against the Aghlabids and Fatamids. Their scale and sophistication overshadow any contemporary military sites in Western Europe.

On the eastern edge of the Carolingian empire, from the late ninth-century mobile bands of Magyar horsemen made inroads that eventually penetrated as far as Lombardy and Provence, prompting an energetic wave of fortress-building in response. From the north, the depredations of marauding Viking armies

3. Debating the European Castral Revolution

Fig. 4. Alcazaba of Almería. Founded in the tenth century, this vast fortification comprised two large walled enclosures and accommodated a royal residence and extensive gardens.

venturing deep inland via navigable river systems were instrumental to the eventual break-up of Carolingian society in the second half of the ninth century. The characteristic Viking fortification of the period was the ditched and embanked enclosure adjacent to a river, as these were naval bases as much as garrisoned camps; among the largest in scale were the enigmatic *longphorts* built on the Irish coast, at least some of which were semi-permanent. Although rulers were initially slow to respond, reciprocal measures included investment in guardposts, fortified bridges and fortifications at river mouths and harbours, as well attested in France, Belgium and the Low Countries. Such initiatives sometimes involved the forced movement of populations, as with the relocation of Quentovic, the principal port in northern France, to the nearby *castrum* of Montreuil-sur-Mer.

Serious though the military actions of Vikings, Saracens and

Magyars were, these events did not cause the rise of the castle. While conflict saw considerable investment in and experimentation with defence-works – by the Carolingian state as well as its enemies – they did not witness the construction of sites we can easily identify as castles. Rather, the weakening of centralised authority created an environment in which fortifications built by noble families ultimately came to flourish. In short, there is no clear 'cause and effect' relationship between increasing levels of insecurity and the origins of the castle, which was a more indirect consequence. If such a relationship existed, we might question why, for instance, the Merovingian period with its well-attested culture of extreme and endemic violence between competing nobles did not see the development of private fortification in the seventh and eighth centuries. The meagre evidence available suggests that Merovingian aristocrats might live in villa complexes enclosed with walls, but this relates to the symbolic definition of property rights rather than defence. Gregory of Tours' sixth-century *Historia Francorum* makes it very clear that the characteristic fortifications of the period were walled former Roman towns, military camps and prehistoric-style forts in naturally defensible positions, rather than proto-castles (Samson 1987).

The chronology of early castle building provides further compelling evidence that the phenomenon was not a simple response to increasing insecurity, although this has not stopped archaeologists and historians caricaturing these sites as inherently military. Across Western Europe as a whole, archaeological evidence has shown us that the real explosion of castle building – in terms of a period that witnessed the steepest increase in the number of private fortifications – occurred in the relatively stable eleventh century, rather than resulting directly from invasions (Higham and Barker 1992: 78-111). Even in the context of the Norman Conquest of England – outwardly one of the most military contexts for early castle building in Western Europe – the real upsurge relates to aristocrats consolidating their positions by fortifying their estate centres. A hypothetical 'national graph' of English castle building therefore sees a short sharp rise in fortification in the decade after 1066 that preceded a more gradual increase to a peak around *c.* 1100 (Eales 1990: 50-1). In this sense, many early castles were part and parcel of a wider pattern of population increase, agricultural expansion, economic investment and urban growth that put a premium on the tighter control of the landscape.

To press this point home with two examples from very different contexts, the great burst of *incastellamento* (the nucleation of villages around hilltop castles: see pp. 140-5) in central Italy occurred from the 920s, after the Saracen depredations had ended following the defeat of the Arabs at Garigliano in 915. Later episodes of Hungarian attack did little to accelerate the process, although *incastellamento* charters sometimes talk of responses to threats and military weaknesses. Instead, the phenomenon represented a ratcheting up of lordly control over landscape and populace for reasons of social control and economic intensification (Wickham 1981: 165-6; Fichtenau 1991: 351). Distribution maps of early castles, necessarily crude as they are, provide us with another angle on the complex interrelationship between encastellation and insecurity. An instructive case in point is Catalonia (Fig. 5), where densities of early castles were highest in the centre of the country – reaching one site per 23km^2 – which was arguably the most secure zone, but low on the borderlands prone to Muslim aggression (Glick 1995: 107).

Many historians and archaeologists have drawn a distinction between the 'public' defences of the eighth and ninth centuries and the 'private' nature of castles. Indeed, this has become something of a foundation-stone in the debate on the origins of the castle. In this sense public authority does not mean communal authority but rather royal provision, with obligations to maintain public fortifications fitting into the framework of service to the state or the monarchy. German medieval historians and castle scholars have stressed the importance of *Befestigungsrecht* ('the right to fortify') in this period, seeing Carolingian-era fortifications as the result of royal policy. The word *Fluchtburg* (refuge castle) is used to

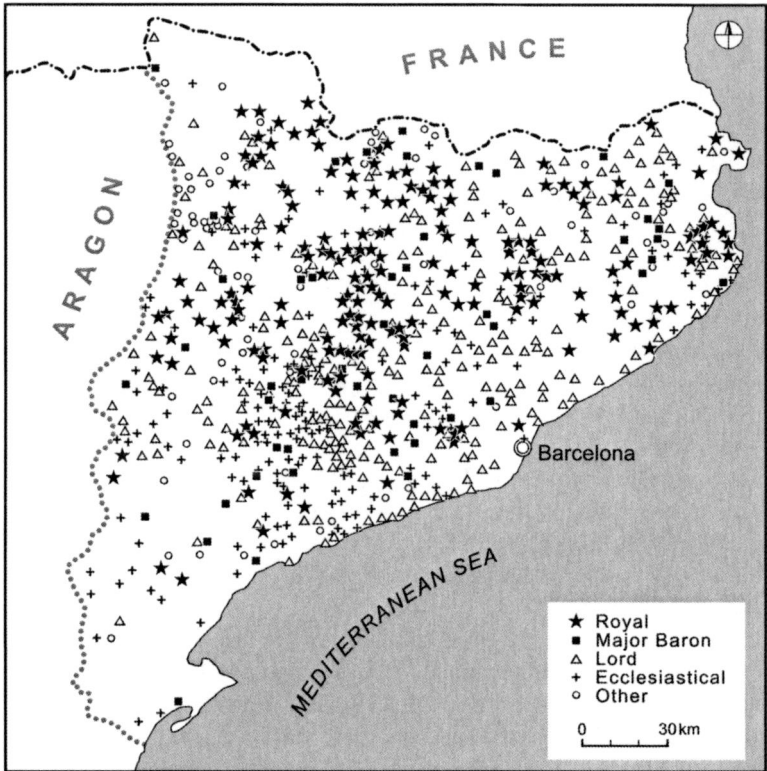

Fig. 5. Encastellation in Catalonia before the mid-fourteenth century, showing the total known distribution of sites and different categories of castle-builders.

describe what might be thought of as quintessential forms of early medieval fortification for sheltering rural populations, in contrast to the later private *Adelsburg* (noble castle). Usually located on hilltops and sometimes entailing the re-fortification of late prehistoric hillforts, many were paired with manorial sites; an illustrative example is the vast eighth-century fortress of Skidrioburg in the district of Lippe. Yet, as we shall see, kings clearly did not enjoy a monopoly over fortress building and we should be careful not to attribute too many otherwise undocumented sites to royal initiative.

3. Debating the European Castral Revolution

A frequently cited source providing supposedly early evidence for some of the first private castles in Europe is Charles the Bald's *Edictum Pistense* (Edict of Pîtres) of 864. In a legislative model that drew on late Roman models of authority, this ordered new defences to be constructed along the Seine but also commanded the destruction of all *castella et firmitates et haias* ('castles, fortifications and enclosures') that had been built without permission. The implications of this order are difficult to gauge, for two reasons. First, it is uncertain whether the phenomenon was specific to the region in question or reflects a wider malaise in other parts of the Carolingian world. Second, while aristocrats had presumably built these fortifications, it is impossible to tell whether these were residences as opposed to temporary defence-works that protected their lands. The importance of this source is that it implies not only the presence of fortifications built as the result of private initiative, but highlights that their existence without royal approval was seen as a threat – not only to rulers, but also to populations that suffered loss and inconvenience from the activities of castellans.

One important way in which we might revise the debate on the origins of the castle is to question how genuine the innovation of 'private' defence represented by the castle really was. The distinction between old 'public' systems of defence that gave way to a new 'private' tradition breaks down at a number of levels. From a longer-term archaeological point of view, private defence had a long ancestry, as demonstrated by the late Roman/Byzantine fortified farmsteads that dotted landscapes in North Africa and the Levant, for example, or the late antique fortified villas well known from areas including Italy, Croatia and Hungary. Similarly, some early castles – especially those built for kings – had underestimated 'public' functions; equally, the first castle-building magnates held public office and their initial campaigns of fortress formed part of their public duty.

Early Norman England provides us with some especially enlightening examples of the overlapping public/private functions of early castles. Reappraisals of eleventh- and twelfth-century great towers including Colchester (Essex) and the Tower of London show that these structures were far less residential than traditionally thought; a major part of their functionality was to serve as stage settings for grand ceremonial gatherings (Goodall 2011: 62-5, 77-81). By the same token, many of the first-generation Norman urban castles superimposed within Anglo-Saxon towns in the 1060s and 70s cannot be conceptualised as 'private' in any real sense, at least in their earliest phases, housing garrisons and serving as focal points in a network of shire government for the new kings (Creighton 2005: 137). Several such sites, including Exeter castle (Devon) and the first Norman fortification on the site of the Tower of London, were laid out in the late eleventh century as 'ringworks' or enclosure castles rather than motte and baileys, using technologies little different to Anglo-Saxon fortifications, and with strategic functions not unlike the final generation of *burhs* built to re-conquer the Danelaw in the tenth century. In this context at least, a binary distinction between 'private' and 'public' fortification misrepresents the complex reality of the Middle Ages.

In general, the emergence of castles was not so much a symptom of social disorder, but of a new form of order, or rather a usurpation of public order by private individuals. The multiplication of castles in the eleventh century in particular might be seen as the result of stability rather than insecurity, and a reflection of a more settled nobility in which wealthy families became tied to power bases within given localities. Even if the location of an individual castle had a strategic character, the private nature of these fortifications meant that they were rarely built as elements within centralised military strategies; in defensive terms they rather served to protect lordly households and to fortify estates. Arguably, social competition was as much a driving force behind early castle building as the need for security, although we should be careful not to over-emphasise the social and symbolic dimensions to early castle building at the expense of military explanations that might be equally valid, if perhaps less fashionable in current scholarship.

3. Debating the European Castral Revolution

Summary

Europe's first castles arose from the social and political trans-
formations of the ninth and tenth centuries that witnessed the
emergence of a 'new aristocracy' with the means and motiva-
tion to defend their homes and estates, compete with their
peers and intimidate communities. The foundation stones of
the traditional 'origins of the castle' argument have been the
underlying belief that the castle's spread was intimately linked
to the growth of feudalism and rooted in France, and a deeply
ingrained conviction that as a 'private fortification' the castle
represented an entirely new species of defence-work. This
model requires urgent revision. Castles did not spread inexora-
bly, creeping mould-like from a heartland to the peripheries of
Europe, but instead evolved in response to specific factors that
varied from area to area. Early European castles had multiple
origins, spanning long periods of time over large areas, while a
rigid distinction between 'private' and 'public' traditions of defence does not represent the reality of the early Middle Ages.

4

Nailing the Valley: Early Towers

One of the great achievements of modern castle study has been to expose the depth and sophistication of symbolism within what can too readily be dismissed as medieval 'military architecture'. Yet much of the debate about the metaphysical qualities of castles to symbolise concepts such as lordship and authority has concerned sites of the later Middle Ages. Easily overlooked is that the builders of early castles equally developed a sophisticated aesthetic repertoire. Accordingly, this chapter explores the roles of the earliest stone castles – in particular great towers – as fortifications but also vehicles for social display, and reflects on possible sources of inspiration for their architecture and planning.

Introducing the European donjon

Multi-storey rectangular or square residential buildings known as *donjons* (derived from the Latin *dominium*, meaning 'lordship') became iconic features of the European landscape in the eleventh and twelfth centuries, with early seminal examples in the tenth. In different parts of Europe we identify these structures more commonly with the term 'great tower' (French *tour maîtresse*; Spanish *torre mayor*; Italian *torre maestro*). Many of the more famous standing structures of the tenth and eleventh centuries lie in northern France, including the iconic sites of Langeais and Loches (both Indre-et-Loire), although it is in the context of Norman England that the largest Romanesque examples are found – both the highest (Rochester, Kent, at 34.5m high including

50

4. Nailing the Valley: Early Towers

its turrets) and the largest in terms of ground plan (Colchester, Essex, at 33.5 x 46.2m) (Goodall 2011: 79, 117-18).

The centrality of the tower to the very idea of the castle is clear: the stone donjon, the timber tower or, in the case of a 'ringwork' or an enclosure castle, the gatehouse, was invariably its focal point. While innovative at the time of their construction, when retained as the visual centrepieces of castles into the later Middle Ages, these remarkable buildings acted as antique symbols of authority. European donjons of the tenth to twelfth centuries are usually square or rectangular in plan; so were those built in the Levant by the Franks, exporting a Western architectural form to mark their lordships rather than adapting Byzantine prototypes. The form was not, however, entirely exclusive to the early castle-building period, to be eclipsed entirely by more complex circular and polygonal structures. The square tower witnessed something of a resurgence in the later medieval period, as exemplified by the royal castle of Vincennes, on the outskirts of Paris, which was re-built in the mid-fourteenth century with an enormous quadrangular donjon (with rounded corner towers) at its core – six storeys and some 51m high, and set within its own moat.

Our sample of standing Romanesque donjons, especially those from before *c.* 1100, is, however, tiny and almost certainly not representative of this building tradition as a whole. Moreover, these sites – iconic as they are – represent an even tinier sample of the entire number of private castles; we should certainly not conflate the debate over the origins of the castle with another about the origins of the great tower or donjon. Another consideration is that while it is entirely correct to think of certain important donjons as influential and 'forward looking' in their designs – somehow anticipating architectural forms and ways of organising space that became more widespread later in time – we should remember that others looked backwards. Equally important to our understanding of the genesis of the European donjon is the notion that the builders and designers of these great structures also drew on the models of ancient structures and the imagery they too conveyed.

Rebuilding Rome: Classical and Carolingian antecedents

In some senses both the concept and architecture of private defence have clear antecedents rooted in the Classical world. Scholars have often drawn upon medieval terminology to describe the private defensive installations of the late Roman period in particular. For example, in his study *Roman Imperial Architecture*, the archaeologist and historian Brian Ward-Perkins styles fortified Byzantine palaces and villas as *châteaux*; the *gasr* (small, square raised forts) of the Libyan frontier as 'castles' of the desert; and the fourth-century country retreat at Pfalzel, near Trier, as resembling a 'keep' (1981: 456-7). While these sorts of terms might be useful to convey certain images to modern-day readers, we should be careful to use the glossary of medieval architecture critically, as the institutions this terminology represents had a social context very specific to the Middle Ages.

The insecurities of the second half of the third century AD saw Roman imperial villas in particular take on an increasingly military aspect, especially in the Balkan-Danube region. Particularly important and influential here are Diocletian's new coastal residence at Split (Croatia) – a fusion between a palatial villa and a military *castrum* encompassed by a rectangular walled circuit studded with monumental gates (Fig. 6) – and Galerius' powerfully fortified palace compound at Gamzigrad (Serbia). The habit of fortifying villas with enclosing walls, turrets and gateways percolated outwards to the Western Empire and North Africa; the same was true of the *praetorium* (the palatial house of a governor or officials) in late antiquity, although such measures were sometimes showy and imitative rather than inspired by security concerns. Evidence for the fortification of late Roman villas and farms is less common in Italy, although archaeologists have identified examples with defensive ditches, towers and even blocked lower-storey windows, while in parts of Gaul and Spain late Roman residences are sometimes found on hilltops, which lent them a defensive aspect (Christie 2006: 460-1).

4. Nailing the Valley: Early Towers

Fig. 6. North gate of Diocletian's palace in Split, Croatia.

Carolingian palaces

The architecture and planning of Carolingian palaces of the eighth and ninth centuries, which in turn drew on Roman and late antique models, provide us with a perceptible source of influence on which early castle-builders seem to have drawn (Fig. 7). A network of perhaps 25 major palaces provided not only centres of luxurious living for itinerant rulers, but also semi-public locations for assemblies and venues for meeting (and impressing) aristocrats. The ascendant view in the long-running debate about whether or not Carolingian palaces were fortified is that those in borderland positions were the exception to the rule in possessing defences, which became an important consideration only with the increasing instability of the ninth century; thereafter a transition from *palatium* to *castrum* is visible in the archaeological record, involving the provision of enclosing defences, defended gateways and towers (Fehring 1991: 132). It is predominantly on the eastern frontiers of the Carolingian Empire that we find the fortified hilltop enclosures whose potentially urban roles historians and archaeologists

53

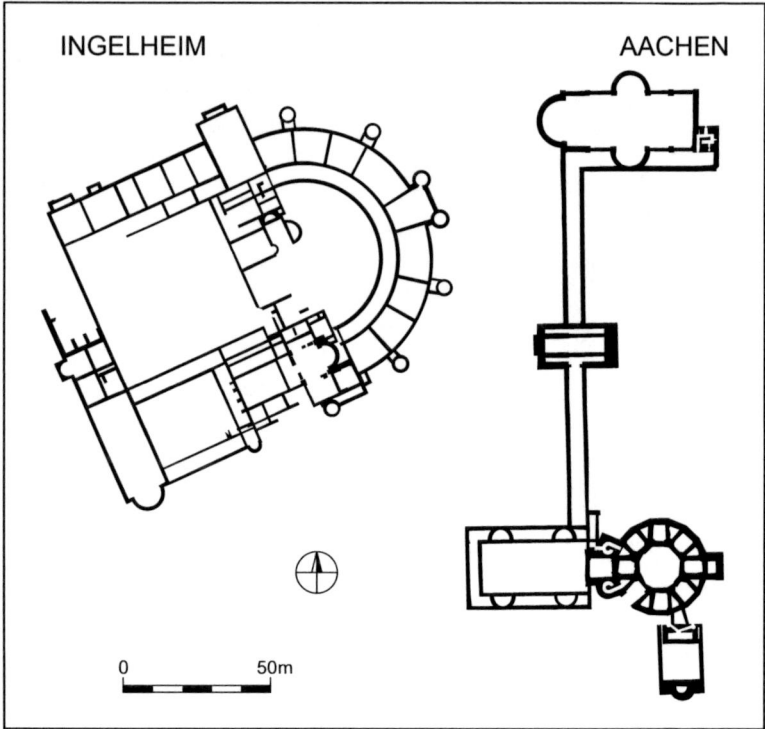

Fig. 7. Plans of Carolingian palaces at Ingelheim and Aachen.

have hotly debated. The *oppidum* known as the Büraberg in northern Hessen (Germany) is a key example that has been subject to detailed archaeological excavation. Comprising a walled hilltop fortress of twelve hectares containing houses and workshops, it was also the seat of a bishop in the mid-eighth century, although whether it equated to an urban or proto-urban centre remains controversial (Henning 2005: 26-9).

The site of Paderborn, in central Germany, supplies us with probably the best known example of a defended Carolingian *Pfalz* (or palace) whose plan has been elucidated by large-scale archaeological excavation. Featuring in Charlemagne's wars against the Saxons from the 770s, agricultural and industrial

4. Nailing the Valley: Early Towers

functions as well as palace buildings were contained within a
fortified enclosure, built first of earth and timber then renewed
in stone. In other cases excavated evidence shows us that
palace 'defences' of the period could be more flashy than real.
At Ingelheim (Fig. 7: left), on the west bank of the Rhine, the
imperial complex was equipped with round towers that projected forward to form a Roman-style façade around the frontal
semi-circular range, although this had little or no genuine
defensive value (there is even a suggestion they contained
latrines!).

Elsewhere, we have very little idea as to the defensive qualities of Carolingian palace sites: at Nijmegen, in Holland, for
instance, Charlemagne constructed a *Pfalz* on a hillock that
was the site of a fourth-century Roman *castrum*. The palace's
layout is unknown, however, as the site was later adapted as a
castle, and it has received little archaeological attention. Some
palaces in Ottonian Germany were certainly fortified; this was
the case with the frontier site of Magdeburg, while at Pfalz
Tilleda, Pfingstberg, where a tenth-century palace on a powerful spur-top position was defended with massive ditches that
subdivided the complex into upper and lower units (Ettel 2008:
170-1). Nonetheless, archaeological and historical evidence
agrees that, as a general rule, defence was not an integral or
primary role of palaces in this period, especially those in the
northern Carolingian heartland. While walled, secure and not
infrequently perpetuating earlier Roman sites, they were often
located in rural positions or semi-detached from towns, with
good links to communications routes but not for any strategic
reason.

Even if we cannot regard palaces of the period as proto-
castles, there is still good reason to think that their designs
were instrumental in inspiring the *idea* of the European donjon. With impressive frontages and, crucially, an emphasis on
multi-storey planning, these monumental complexes embody
the same hallmarks of display and the hierarchical division of
space through three dimensions that characterised the great
towers of the eleventh and twelfth centuries. Another point of

comparison is that Carolingian rulers drew on Classical imagery through the architecture of their palaces to bolster their positions in the same way that early castle builders recycled antique fabric in their halls and donjons, as we shall see (p. 76). It is well known, for instance, that the builders of Charlemagne's palaces at Aachen and Ingelheim plundered, imported and re-used Roman *spolia* as antique adornments and part of a repertoire of Classical imagery at the Carolingian court, while the palace at Frankfurt am Main stood on the site of a Roman *castellum*.

At Aachen, in north-west Germany, the famous palace built for Charlemagne at the epicentre of the Carolingian world towards the end of the eighth century featured a substantial rectangular building of *c.* 15 x 30m that interrupted an impressive double storey gallery between the great hall to the north and the palace-church complex to the south (Fig. 7: right). Traditionally viewed as a grand entranceway, an alternative interpretation sees it containing imperial living quarters in an upper storey, with the elevated hall at Frankfurt am Main offering a likely parallel (Lobbedey 2003). Another towered structure within the complex at Aachen was the *Granusturm*, set against the back of the great hall and containing a stair and a series of vaulted rooms. The lower 20m of the structure is original Carolingian fabric, representing a remarkable survival of the period (Fig. 8).

The mid-ninth-century royal palace at Naranco, near Oviedo in Spain, is another famous and potentially influential palace structure of the period, although from the rather different context of the kingdom of Asturia. Its famous open *solarium* at the end of an elevated hall may reference late antique models and, in turn, bears comparison to aspects of later donjon architecture, as does the double converging flight of stairs on the structure's exterior. High-status use of upper-storey space was a defining characteristic of Carolingian royal complexes more generally, as were features of planning such as audience chambers and a panoply of showy architectural trappings such as arcaded or colonnaded galleries, entrance-ways and even balconies.

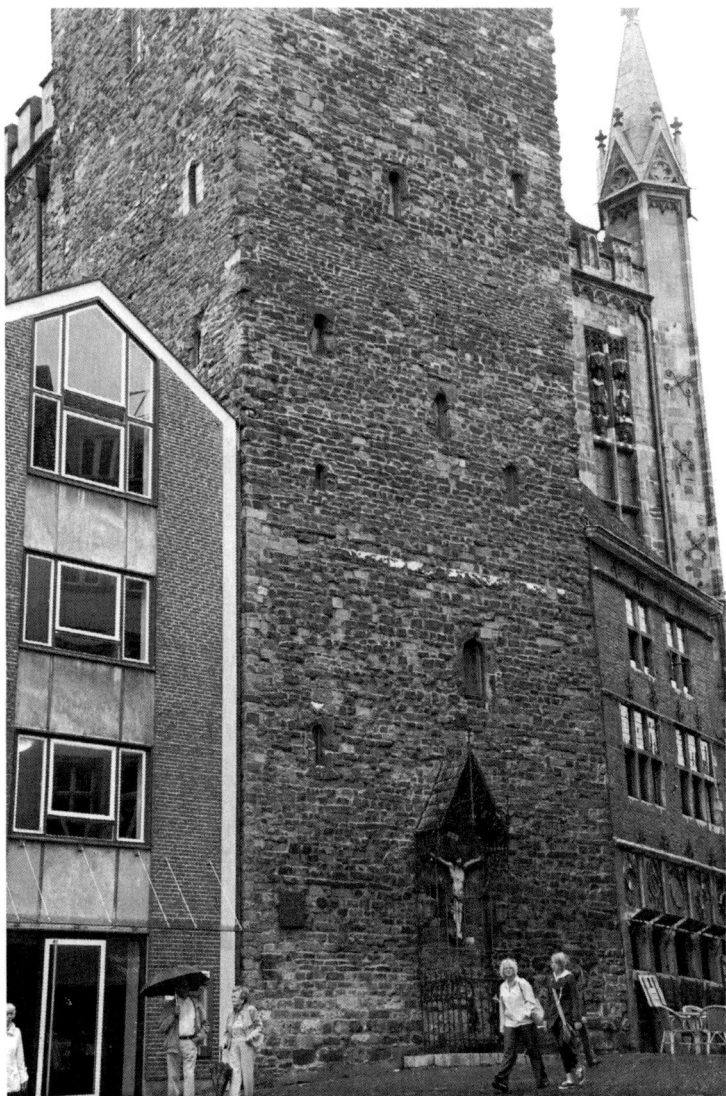

Fig. 8. The late eighth-century *Granusturm* at Aachen. The lower portions of the tower contain Carolingian masonry although the building it is attached to is a neo-Gothic structure of the 1840s, on the site of Charlemagne's hall.

Another element integral to the Carolingian-era palace template was the twinning of domestic and administrative facilities with a prominent church or chapel, which in a case such as Aachen projected beyond the palace façade so that the 'westwork' presented an extraordinary show-front for public audiences. Comparable architectural forms are also apparent in monastic planning of the period. At Lorsch, in Germany, a remarkable monastic gatehouse of the late eighth or early ninth century preserves an upper-floor hall above an arcaded lower level that emulates Roman triumphal-style arches and shows innovation at the interface between military and ecclesiastical building traditions. When later emulated by the nobility, this repertoire represented the essential basis for the medieval donjon. The genius of the idea was to resolve the contradictory needs of privacy and public display within a structure that proclaimed social separateness but also allowed access for subjects to be regulated and controlled depending upon status.

Early European donjons: plans and functions

For a long period, mainstream studies of the Romanesque tended to marginalise donjons as the embodiment of 'military architecture', focusing instead on ecclesiastical buildings. As we are seeing, however, the distinction between military and ecclesiastical architecture was not at all clear-cut in the period under consideration, and new research on the designs and plans of great towers is moving us away from the time-honoured image of the 'keep' as a forbidding and austere stronghold of last resort (Marshall 2002b). The classic donjon integrated the hall, chamber and chapel in one unified conception, and surviving examples preserve sophisticated multi-level plans that channelled movement and conditioned the experience of architectural space in ways that their builders consciously intended to impress and perhaps astonish visitors. The finest structures deployed an array of decorative Romanesque elements to stunning aesthetic effect. In the more elaborate examples arcading

– both 'blind' against walls and 'open' to give a colonnade-style effect – drew the observer's attention to selected areas of the interior and exterior; pilaster buttresses emphasised the verticality of the tower; and external 'appearance' doorways at upper levels resembled balconies from which the lord could appear in front of assembled audiences.

The magnificent early eleventh-century donjon at Loches exemplifies many of these themes (Fig. 9). Comprising three stories above a basement, the status of the building tangibly increased as the visitor ascended, with schemes of decoration on features such as doorways indicating differential status. The presence of a forebuilding (or *petit donjon*: an attached projection, usually rectangular, that enclosed the entrance way and carried a stair) provided an additional means of controlling access arrangements. At Loches, as elsewhere, it allowed a carefully staged approach and a theatrical grand entrance, perhaps taking inspiration from the *porticus*-type of Carolingian palaces. Other indicators that a donjon such as Loches was built at least in part for ceremonial purposes include the provision of a reception area in advance of a magnificently lit hall, and a startling absence of security measures – of all the doors in the structure only the main door into the forebuilding could be barred (Marshall 2002a: 143-5). Another way in which different storeys signalled ascending status was where ground floor entrances provided access to either reception rooms or lower halls, which linked in turn to more privileged upper halls, as apparent in late tenth- and early eleventh-century structures at Tours (Indre-et-Loire) and the *Castrum* d'Andone (Charente).

From the outside, the finely dressed and coursed ashlar faces and pilaster buttresses (tall external columns of masonry) of the donjon at Loches emphasise its striking verticality. That these were quite thin suggests that their utility value (i.e. bearing loads) was minimal; either flat or semi-circular in form, when regularly spaced and rising from bottom to top they were unmistakably showy architectural features. Some may even have been skeuomorphs – ornamental facsimiles of timber

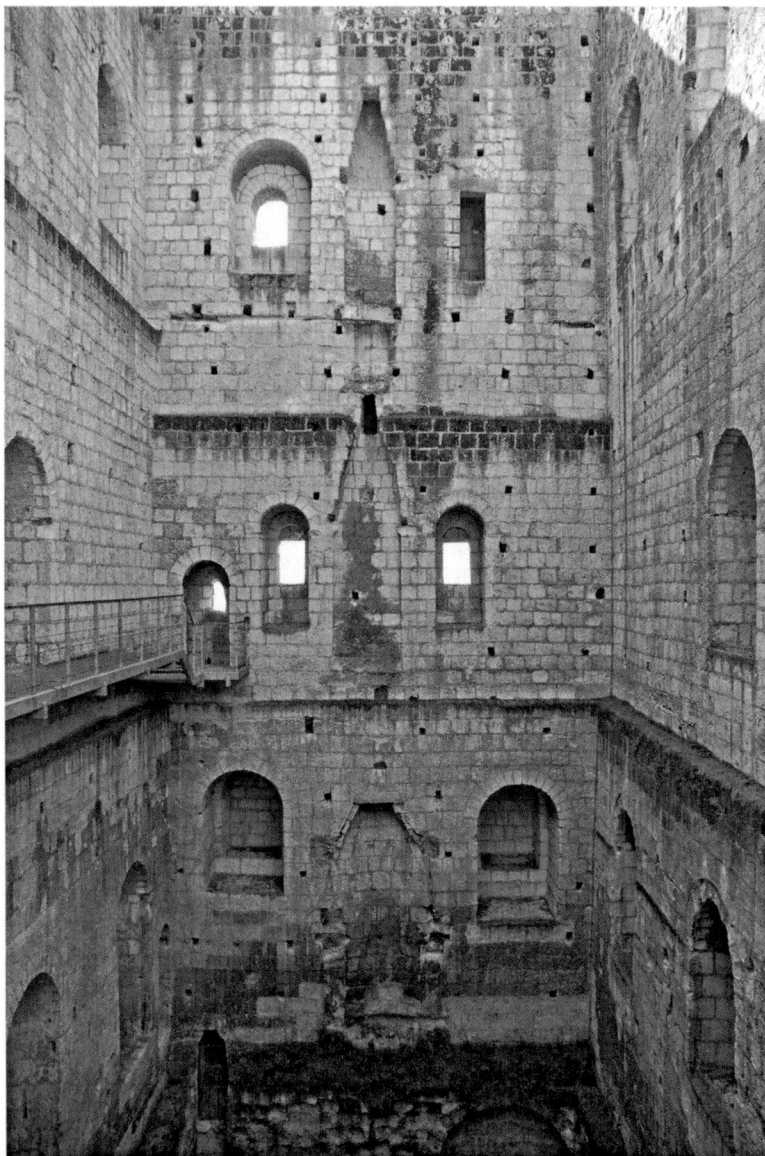

Fig. 9. Donjon of Loches.

architecture – lending otherwise 'cutting edge' buildings a retro flavour. Loches also exhibits the placement of a chapel at an upper level directly over the entranceway, offering spiritual protection. Religious symbolism could also be represented in other ways, as at Trim (Co. Meath), Ireland's largest donjon (of *c.* 1200), where the building's planning as a cross-shape ensured military weakness but likely carried Christian connotations (O'Keeffe 2001: 76).

In France as well as in England there is growing acceptance that above all the donjon was a deliberately visible statement of seigneurial power (Mesqui 1991: 96-105). A hierarchy of donjons existed, from enormous quasi-palatial complexes with 'double pile' plans (i.e. with four rooms at each level) to modest *tours-beffrois* comprising simple vertical arrangements of single spaces. Structures across this spectrum were active at any single point in time from the tenth century onwards, emphasising that donjons neither evolved nor diffused in simple fashion. At either end of the hierarchy of donjons there is good reason to think that that residential accommodation was not a primary function; a crucial role of most royal and ducal examples was to host public ceremonies, while the most modest seigneurial towers were unheated and could not have functioned as domestic spaces in any meaningful way. The unifying factor is display; the type of donjon termed as 'marker towers', somewhere in the middle of this hierarchy, is particularly demonstrative, comprising tall and narrow structures rising from residential complexes, as at Montbrun (Haute-Vienne, France) (Marshall 2002a: 33).

The notion of the tower 'nailing the valley' (Thompson 1991: 23) encapsulates the important figurative roles of these structures. A tower was an unmistakable presence – an elevated and iconic architectural feature that forcefully stamped the seigneurial mark on the locality (Fig. 10). Expensive and omnipresent but also exclusive and inaccessible, they acted as permanent visual reminders in stone of the lordly presence, even when their owners and builders were not in residence. By the same token, the slighting and desecration of a donjon could in certain instances mark the discontinuity of lordship. Concepts of noble legitimacy feature prominently in eleventh- and twelfth-century chroniclers' accounts of castle spaces. Particularly instructive is the legend recounted by Benoît of Ste-Maure (*c.* 1150) of Arlette's entry into the castle of Falaise (Calvados), in which the mother of the future William the Conqueror was permitted to access the donjon via its ceremonial main entrance only upon the realisation that she was pregnant with him (Hicks 2009: 57-8).

Keen to expose the lineage of the great tower, architectural historians have searched for stylistic comparisons and lines of descent, particularly from northern France to other parts of Europe, including Norman England. A particularly noteworthy development is that the ancestry of London's great White Tower, with its 'double pile' plan, can now be traced to Ivry-de-Bataille (Eure), a structure of around AD 1000 (Impey 2008: 240). While crucial to the study of these remarkable buildings, family trees of donjon development and typologies of their forms should not obscure the individuality that they expressed in their medieval settings. Certainly, forms of tower-building in Normandy did not necessarily form ready-made templates for castles in late eleventh- and early twelfth-century England. For instance, in some senses Caen castle might be thought of as the quintessential 'Norman castle' – the centrepiece of ducal authority over the fortified town and Normandy itself on the eve of the Conquest. Yet William the Conqueror's eleventh-century fortress here did not possess a donjon and did not take the form of a motte and bailey. Rather, it comprised a compact palace within an expansive masonry enceinte, much like the contemporary ducal enclosure castle at Fécamp; Caen's donjon was an addition of the twelfth century, its construction one phase in a complex sequence of rebuilding clarified by Michel du Boüard's excavations from the late 1960s (Decaëns and Dubois 2009).

The German equivalent of the donjon was the *Bergfried* (Fig. 11). Comprising a round, rectangular or square tower, usually entered at the first- or second-floor level, the *Bergfried* differed

4. Nailing the Valley: Early Towers

Fig. 10. Le Château d'Albon: a small seigneurial donjon overlooking the Rhône valley.

from the French and English style of great tower in one crucial respect: its marked lack of domestic qualities. This has often resulted in their perception as last redoubts and an unfortunate translation into English as 'watchtowers'. Many were partnered by a separate domestic block (the *Palas*), with the two elements integrated in castle planning only from the fourteenth century onwards. The first tower on the site of the Turmberg, near Karlsruhe-Durlach, dated archaeologically to

Fig. 11. German *Bergfriede:* (left) the Juliusturm, in Spandau citadel (only the lowermost masonry is original), Berlin; (right) Rothenfels in Bavaria.

the late eleventh century, is a particularly early example of a rectangular tower; more typically these features date to the mid-twelfth century, as at Königswinter (Rhein-Sieg-Kreis) and Rothenfels (Main-Spessart) (Fig. 11: right). Exemplars of the circular *Bergfriede* of *c.* 1200 or before that were particularly characteristic of central and northern Germany include Burg Anhalt near Quedlinburg and the Juliusturm in Spandau, west of Berlin (Fig. 11: left), although the distribution of round towers with Romanesque traits also extends into eastern France and, to the north, parts of Denmark and Sweden.

Reconstructing the original appearances of *Bergfriede* can be problematic, however, given the propensity of nineteenth-century German restorers to medievalise and militarise these structures to bolster the political power and social influence of aristocratic families, showing how the castle image retained currency and continued to be re-shaped. Typically bereft of

4. Nailing the Valley: Early Towers

trappings of luxurious living such as fireplaces and windows, the tall, narrow and visually striking medieval *Bergfried* – more 'look at' than 'look out' – was no less an emblem of lordship than the donjon or great tower, and while we must not deny their defensive roles entirely, new approaches are defining these buildings in a more balanced way (Thompson 1991: 22-4; Zeune 1996: 45).

A recent re-interpretation of the twin circular *Bergfriede* within Muenzenberg castle (Hess) illustrates this well. The austere east tower, some 29m high and originally lit by a single window, was located some distance from the gate, whose defence it could not contribute to, instead forming part of a 'show façade' that symbolised the elevation and quasi-noble status of its builder, Kuno I von Muenzenberg in the mid-twelfth century (Jost 2002: 181-2). Another key aspect to the symbolism of these remarkable edifices, particularly those in towns, is that they rivalled church towers in terms of visual dominance on the urban skyline. They would have proclaimed to populations the emergence of the nobility as rival power-holders to the church, especially where erected in the immediate vicinity of ecclesiastical towers. Ecclesiastical lords also built towers of their own: at Soest and Xanten, both in north-west Germany, the Archbishops of Cologne constructed early towered residences next to important churches in the tenth century, but in other instances their construction by the nobility might have been deliberately provocative.

Great towers were rare in the medieval landscapes of Scandinavia, although an important early exception is the circular Bastrup Tower in Zealand – one of the largest European donjons of all, founded in the twelfth century, perhaps by the powerful Hvide family (Randsborg 2003). Some 21m in diameter and with walls 6m thick, this unusually massive structure may well have exceeded 30m in height, although only the base remains and little is known of the wider complex within which it must have stood. The tower's dramatic setting suggests that Danish rulers too were consciously buying into the idea of a quintessential European hilltop castle: it was built on a lakeside cliff-top, looming above an expanse of open water and with a vista suggesting that visual impact and aesthetic sensibility were critical in its conception.

We should be careful to remember that these early great towers do not in themselves equate to castles, however. The mistake is easily made: medieval chroniclers in the eleventh and twelfth centuries often identified individual castles by reference to their towers, although their sites would have been more complex entities taking up far larger areas of space. While great towers were the most recognisable and iconic elements within early private fortifications, they did not themselves represent the full range of functions that these places served. The problem is compounded by the building-focused approaches that castellologists have usually taken. While the architecture of most of the more important early donjons has been well studied and their domestic planning is the focus of energetic enquiry, their contexts in many cases remain obscure, partly because their sites have in most cases been redeveloped through the centuries.

Points of origin: innovation and emulation

Architectural historians have long debated the origins of great towers, although archaeology is playing an increasingly critical role in re-evaluating when and where the earliest examples were built, not least because of the growing application of absolute dating techniques. One of the very earliest known secular stone towers in Europe was built at Doué-la-Fontaine (Fig. 12; also known as *La Chapelle*), in the Loire valley in northern France, as revealed by painstaking excavations in 1967-70 (De Boüard 1973-4). Crucially, it was built not as a single integrated structure but developed from an earlier princely hall (*salle d'apparat*) constructed around *c.* 900 (datable, it should be emphasised, using traditional techniques). This single-storey rectangular building, with a ground plan of 23 x 16m, featured two doors, at least one window, and was apparently capped with a thatched roof. A radical re-build of *c.* 950 transformed it into a towered lordly residence by blocking

4. Nailing the Valley: Early Towers

Fig. 12. Doué-la-Fontaine: a Carolingian hall-house converted into a tower and later encased within a motte, as revealed by excavation in the late 1960s.

the ground floor openings and adding an additional habitable storey accessible via a timber scaffold-type structure. Theobald the Trickster, Count of Blois, is a likely perpetrator of this development. A third phase, around *c.* 1000, saw the structure surrounded by a ditch and encased within a motte, and while it seems likely that at least one further level was added, there is no direct evidence for this. Fulk Nerra, Count of Anjou, used the tower as a prison following its capture in 1026, although it was disused by the time of his death in 1040 and superseded by another motte nearby. A remarkable survival at the site is the elaborate religious pictorial graffiti scratched into the plaster of the lower storey when it was blocked and used as a jail, the complexity of the iconography pointing towards the internment of a clerical or other learned prisoner (Kupfer 2011).

De Boüard's classic excavation at Doué-la-Fontaine has sometimes been used as evidence not only that the Loire region was an initial hotspot from which donjons diffused, but that it is some type of experimental 'prototype', with the origins of the donjon inherently related to a process of technological innovation. In the opening chapter of his hugely influential *English Castles*, R. Allen Brown wrote that at Doué 'we seem to be in the very presence of the events we seek', meaning the origin of the castle (1976: 8). To understand the donjon as a technical accomplishment misunderstands its essential symbolic value, however, as towers were, after all, neither militarily the most effective buildings not ideal in domestic terms given issues of access and lighting.

Fulk Nerra, Count of Anjou (987-1040), is celebrated as one of Europe's premier castle-builders of this critical period (Anderson 1970: 45-6), commissioning numerous castles – often dramatically situated on promontories – to bolster and expand his power base in the region against his chief rivals, the counts of Blois (Fig. 13). In the case of Beaugency (Loiret) (Fig. 14), built on the borderlands between these two spheres of influence, it is unclear who the builder was, although the structure is now dated to the early eleventh century and thus the period of Fulk's campaigns (Impey 2008: 230-1). Recent re-dating of the aforementioned example of Loches through dendrochronology (tree-ring dating) similarly attributes this structure to Fulk Nerra, near the end of his reign. Previously the donjon was usually attributed to the early twelfth century on stylistic grounds, on the mistaken assumption that secular buildings must inevitably lag behind ecclesiastical ones. Dendrochronological analysis of samples of timber from original scaffolding in 'putlog' holes, lintels over doors and beams at different storeys is sufficiently precise to cast light on the time needed to realise such a creation: the first level was started in the autumn/winter of 1012/13 and the third level completed by *c.* 1035 (Dormoy 1997).

We should always treat such evidence with care; in cases where scientific dating results do not fit our preconceptions, alternative interpretations are possible. At Sainte-Suzanne (Mayenne), a donjon usually thought to have been built by the Viscounts of Maine in the second half of the eleventh century, a programme of radiocarbon dating revealed tenth-century dates

4. Nailing the Valley: Early Towers

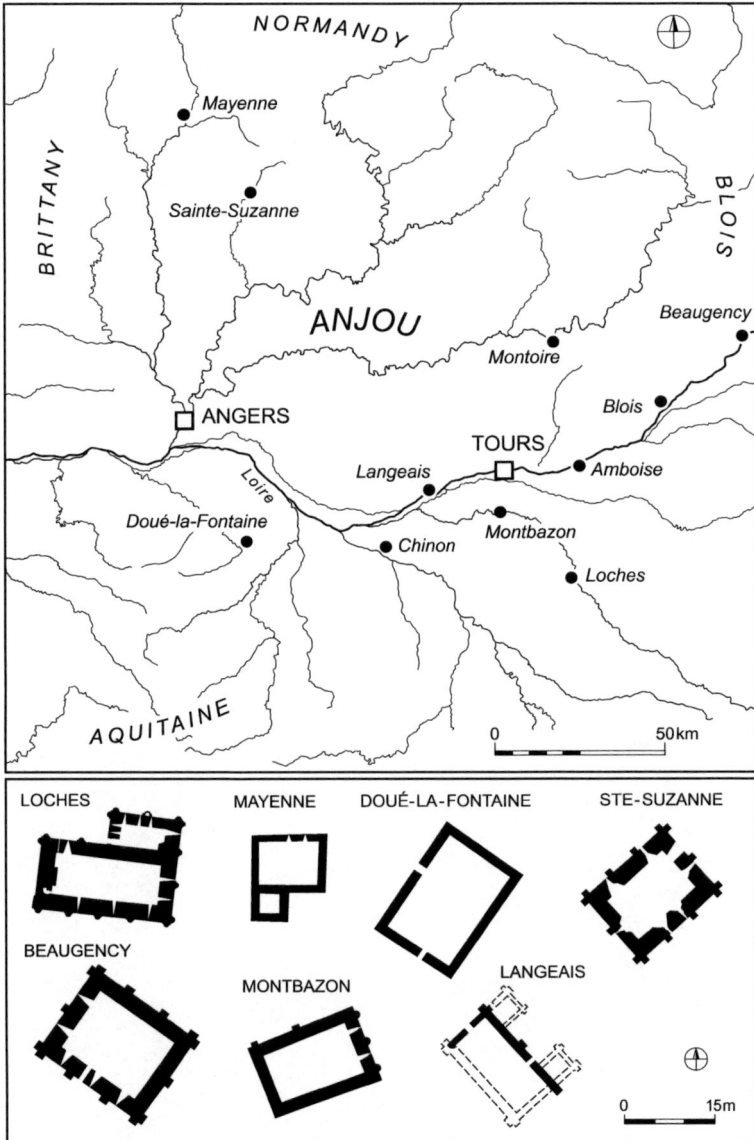

Fig. 13. Early donjons in and around Anjou, France. Some of the structures are depicted in plan form.

69

Fig. 14. Beaugency: an early eleventh-century donjon, later heightened.

that are inconceivably early; the likely explanation here is that its builders re-used timbers from a timber tower on the site (Renoux 2010: 25). Applying the science of absolute dating to donjons need not always push construction dates back in time. Thermoluminescence offers exciting new potential, but bricks from the donjon at Avranches (Manche) produced dates in the second half of the twelfth century and the first half of the thirteenth century. These clearly relate to a reconstruction of the north-east tower, meaning that the research question of whether the original building was a potential source of influence for the sort of double-pile plan seen at London's White Tower and Ivry-de-Bataille went unanswered (Bouvier et al. 2011).

We nonetheless need to be careful on several fronts about equating Fulk Nerra's famous towers with the origins of castles. Painstakingly systematic mapping of early donjons known through documentary references but sometimes without surviving physical evidence on the ground reveals a more complex pattern than a diffusion of this architectural form from the contested region in and around Anjou. The impression of the Loire as a seminal locus of early donjon building is clearly accentuated by the better survival rate of these structures relative to other parts of northern France. If anything, a more obvious cradle of early donjon building is the Île-de-France, where chroniclers record the existence of several towers by the mid-tenth century, mainly with no surviving traces, although the problems of how reliably we can interpret references to *turres* and similar words are covered elsewhere (pp. 33-4). It should be emphasised that most of these references mention the towers in the context of unusual events – primarily sieges, but also imprisonments – rather than dating their construction; among the more convincing are mentions of towers in the area north-east of Paris at Château-Thierry (Aisne) and Compiègne (Oisne), while at Coucy and Laon (both Aisne) it is difficult to judge whether references to towers within towns or cities were independent units or effectively extensions to urban defences (Impey 2008: 228-9).

We should also be very careful not to confuse the origins of the donjon with the origin of the castle, either as an institution or as a physical reality. It is clear that in some cases Fulk Nerra's castles were in effect redevelopments of established lordship centres that already combined defensive uses and strategic potential with administrative, residential and other functions; many also developed incrementally, as the example of Doué-la-Fontaine testifies. A prime example is Loches, which was not raised on a greenfield site but represented an addition to an extant fortified centre developed by Fulk's father, Geoffrey Greymantle, complete with a collegiate church and an adjoining market settlement (Bachrach 1993: 102). The tower also stands on the site of an earlier motte that was partly removed and lowered to take its enormous weight; this early fortification clearly guarded the natural promontory site, reminding us that earth and timber as well as stone fortifications were used in the power plays between Anjou and Blois (Aarts 1996: 18-21). The donjon was, therefore, not a new seigneurial presence in its own right, rather embodying a different personality of lordship with a more visible public face.

Changing interpretations of the donjon at Langeais (Indre-et-Loire) provide a further instructive case study. Rectangular in plan and with base dimensions of 16 x 7m, this spur-top building of *c.* 1000 has something of the character of a residential hall as much as a tower *per se* (Fig. 13: bottom). A detailed re-evaluation based on stone-by-stone analysis has shed new light on the structure's date, phasing, planning and functions, yet many aspects of its setting remain obscure (Impey and Lorans 1998). For example, it seems highly likely but difficult to prove both that the tower was a component part of a larger building, of stone or timber, to which was attached a larger bailey-like unit containing a collegiate chapel (Saint-Sauveur, elements of which survive). Other aspects of the castle's early plan remain more obscure still. It is unclear if there is also an early motte on the site (an earthwork near the donjon has sometimes been identified as one – perhaps a motte *avancée* – but it is small and has never been excavated), or whether the

4. Nailing the Valley: Early Towers

putative court around the chapel pre-dated the donjon. The heavily wooded nature of the site today and the fact that it was redeveloped as a fifteenth-century château mean that such questions are likely to remain unanswered. This example brings into focus, once again, the methodological challenges of understanding early great towers in their wider contexts.

A further consideration is that while it is tempting to see the early European donjon as a sparkling and newfangled creation at the cutting edge of technology, these buildings did not represent an entirely new phenomenon. The European landscape was already studded with ecclesiastical towers with which builders had experimented in previous centuries. In short, the idea of the tower was not new; the critical departure was the idea of living in one – or at least giving the appearance of doing so, as in many cases there is good reason to think that owners were accommodated elsewhere. Meanwhile, there is good reason to think that the imagery of the donjon was intended to hark back to the Roman past as much as to appear something new and different. Fulk Nerra was characterised as 'neo-Roman consul' in Bachrach's (1993) political biography. He drew on antique traditions in royal ceremonies, law and in military organisations and celebrations; it is only natural that castles were part and parcel of this neo-Roman image-making. Having made several pilgrimages to the Holy Land, Fulk Nerra would also have been well aware of Byzantine and Roman architectural heritage.

Archaeological work is throwing up new examples of early donjons in unexpected contexts. Most dramatic of these is the case of the Château de Mayenne in north-west France (Fig. 15). Conservation works in the late 1990s unveiled one of Western Europe's earliest standing secular buildings, dating to the tenth century, encased within a much later and heavily re-built castle that was modified as a prison in the nineteenth century (Early 1998; 2002). Mayenne is worth considering closely, not just as an exceptionally early fortified residence, built by the Carolingian king and/or the Counts of Maine, but as a model for the integration of archaeological, architectural and documentary research. Progressing hand in hand with a major programme of building conservation, this wide-ranging project has now made the early remains intelligible to the public through imaginative presentation in a museum on the site.

Mayenne was the site of an episcopal *villa* of the seventh/eighth century, and the earliest castle was built on an elevated riverside position that suggestively preserves evidence of an underlying post-built building. The structure comprised two elements: a rectangular *corps de logis* (or principal block) of three levels, and an adjoining *tour carée* (or square turret) that rose above it. The building was flanked by two terraces or galleries, perhaps carrying porticoes; it lay within a defended enclosure, first of earth and timber and later stone, and was evidently one component of a larger complex. The main block comprised a basement for storage, accessible internally via a wooden stair and lit only by narrow windows; a first floor level, featuring a row of large and impressive round-headed windows in the north wall and plastered within, which was evidently an impressive semi-public reception hall; and an upper storey perhaps used as a retiring space.

The weight of evidence from radiocarbon dating, pottery, coins and the scant documentation, makes a compelling case for a construction date of *c.* 900. Comparisons are impossible given that virtually no other Carolingian buildings survive in anything like the same state of preservation, although it is unlikely to have been unique. The complex may have had a strategic context in the tenth century, lying near the border with Brittany, although its plan and the thinness of the walls (*c.* 1.3m) surely rule out a primarily military role. A particularly striking feature of its design is the selective re-use of Roman building materials, including a façade of huge granite slabs transported from the nearby Gallo-Roman fortress at Jublains. Mayenne's builders were also harnessing and re-using the power of the Roman past in other ways. The conscious revival of Roman architectural traditions is suggested by the style of single and double semi-circular brickwork arches in the tower but also by a stunning range of windows that flooded the

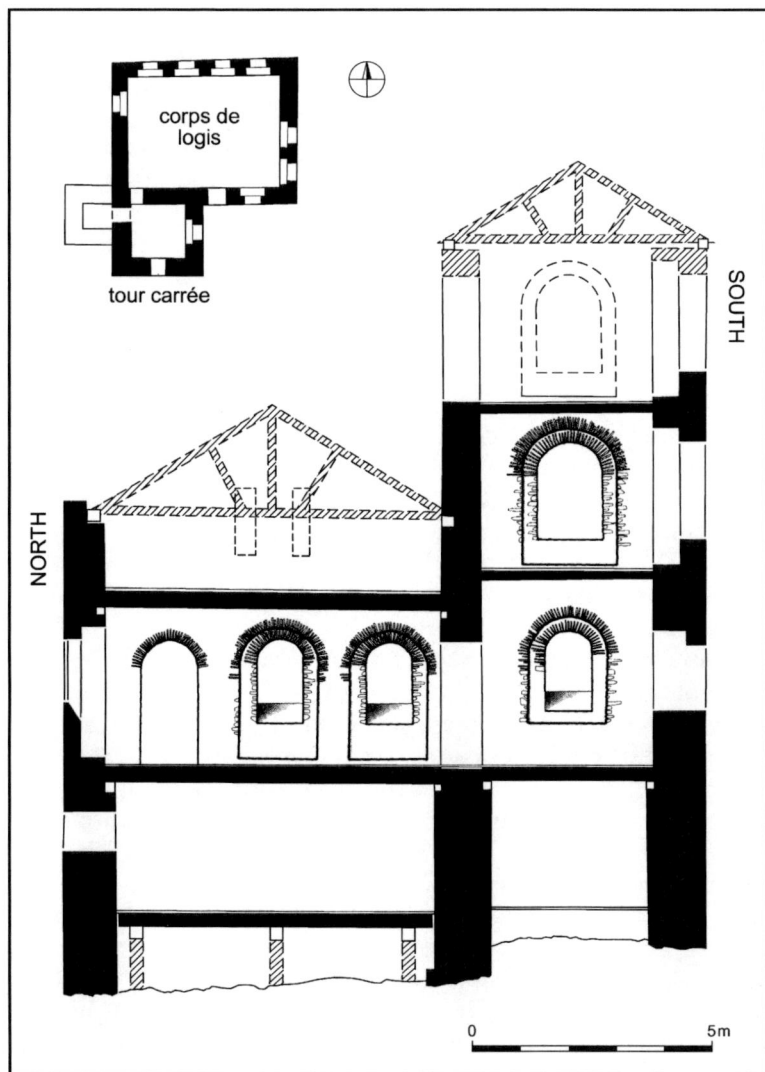

Fig. 15. Château de Mayenne, showing the plan and elevation of a Carolingian castle.

hall with light (and would also have further compromised its defensibility), and by the use of Roman-style pink mortar containing crushed brick to create a render. It is unlikely that lords were emulating Roman structures directly; rather, they were buying into a mélange of Carolingian models, and memories of rulers who themselves actively used and manipulated the heritage of *romanitas*.

Re-use of Roman building materials within early donjons is also testified widely in England and Wales, most famously at Colchester (Essex) and Chepstow (Monmouthshire), where brick and tile were incorporated into late eleventh-century great towers. More widely in medieval Europe the custom of polychrome masonry referenced imperial architecture. At Kaiserwerth in Germany, for example, Frederick Barbarossa's late twelfth-century castle on the site of a Carolingian palace made use of columns of black basalt and white tufa to dramatic effect (Fig. 16). From approximately the same period Henry II's donjon at Dover (Kent, England) made essentially similar allusions to Classical heritage, but here through horizontally banded stonework.

A final consideration is that our understanding of the origins of great towers probably focuses excessively on sites at the summit of the social spectrum. Lords of more modest means were building equivalent sites, including the *roccas* of Italy and southern France. An illustrative site is Niozelles (Alpes-de-Haute-Provence, France) (Fig. 17), where excavation has clarified a neat sequence of early castle building of modest scale (Mouton 2008). Around 970-80 the site comprised a multistorey house with attached courtyard, perched prominently on a hilltop but otherwise undefended. Its redevelopment as a castle can be dated closely to *c.* 980-90, as a 'ritual' deposit in the form of a pottery vessel containing a coin was buried among the foundations that were to form the north-west angle of a rectangular donjon. Set on an enlarged platform, the tower was surrounded by a polygonal walled enclosure, making it defensible and transforming the site into a visually striking multi-tiered edifice, although occupied as a

4. Nailing the Valley: Early Towers

Fig. 16. Kaiserwerth: vertical bands of different masonry in a twelfth-century imperial palace or *Pfalz* on the banks of the Rhine.

castle for no longer than 40 years and a transient feature of the Provençal landscape.

It is similarly the impact on the locality of a relatively modest seigneurial family that the architecture and planning of the Château d'Albon (Drôme) (Fig. 10) proclaims, as unveiled by an important archaeological project commenced in 1993 (Barry et al. 2001). The austere but visually prominent motte-top donjon represents the tip of an iceberg that several seasons of painstaking excavation by an international team has melted away to reveal a longer-term sequence of seigneurial occupation mantled by the earthworks. By the tenth century a lordly complex focused on a chapel and accompanying post-built structure with large numbers of grain silos around it was enclosed within a defensive rampart. A second phase, dated to the late eleventh/early twelfth century, saw the rebuilt chapel accompanied by an impressive hall with a private chamber, with the motte and three-storey tower a later development of the thirteenth century, reminding us that these iconic struc-

Phase 1: *c.*970-80

entrance?

outbuilding

granary

Phase 2: *c.*980-90

entrance?

doorway

hearth

north
annexe

donjon

waste pit

south-west
annexe

hearth

south
annexe

0   5m

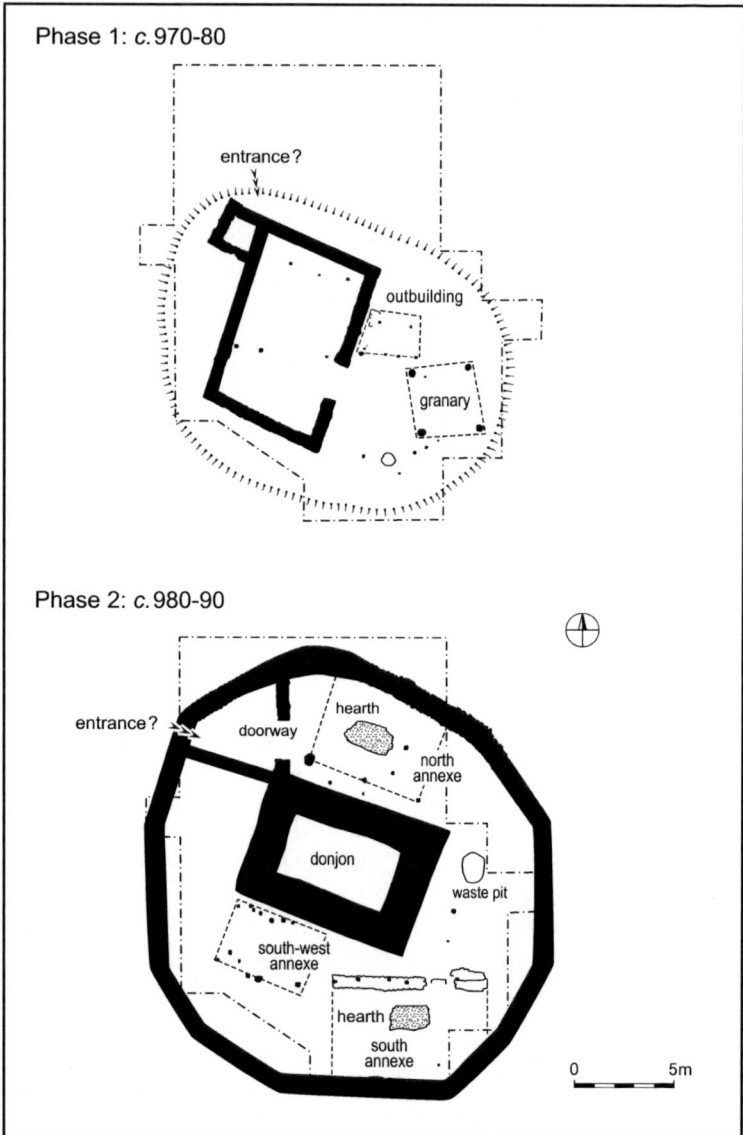

Fig. 17. Niozelles: transformation of a hilltop house into a donjon within a curtain wall in the late tenth century.

4. Nailing the Valley: Early Towers

tures were component parts in wider complexes that in some cases developed piecemeal over several centuries before the 'classic' motte and bailey form was attained.

The Anglo-Saxon heritage: burhs *and* burh-geats

Although much of the foregoing discussion has concerned early donjons in France, we can identify other significant antecedents to masonry castle architecture of the eleventh and twelfth centuries. One of the most intriguing and controversial of these is the tradition of fortified estate centres built for members of the thegnly (or noble) classes in late Anglo-Saxon England. Historians have frequently cited the statement in Orderic Vitalis' early twelfth-century *Historia ecclesiastica* that the Norman Conquest was aided by the fact that castles were scarcely known in the English provinces as 'proof' that private defences did not exist in the period, although a more nuanced interpretation suggests that the chronicler may have been making a specific allusion to William the Conqueror's Northumbrian campaign of 1068 (Coulson 1996: 172). While there is no escaping the fact that educated contemporaries saw the castles of the Norman Conquest and colonisation as intrinsically different from the residences and defences of the English nobility, we need no longer see these sorts of sites as somehow unusual or odd.

A major advance is that the Anglo-Saxon *burh* need not always represent an expansive communal fortification. Ann Williams (1992; 2008: 88-90) has shown how possession of a 'bell-house and *burh-geat*' was part of a package of attributes that the well known Anglo-Saxon 'promotion law' required of a thegn and that these comprised the small-scale defence-works of lords. The most important sites among the handful of known archaeological correlates are Goltho (Lincolnshire) and Sulgrave (Northamptonshire), where compact defensive enclosures around pre-Norman halls and ancillary buildings have been identified, although uncertainties over dating make both sites intensely problematic and in neither case was the critical gate located.

Fig. 18. Earls Barton: a likely example of an Anglo-Saxon thegnly enclosure incorporating an estate church.

It is clear that a tower would have been the focal point of these thegnly sites – a gate tower set into the rampart, the belfry of a chapel or church lying nearby, or feasibly some sort of hybrid. All Saints Church at Earls Barton, in Northamptonshire (Fig. 18), provides the most illustrative example, internationally famous for its turriform nave dating from as far back as *c.* 1000 and probably earlier, complete with ornate pilaster-work on its flashy exterior. The tower rises on a locally prominent natural spur and a large defensive earthwork lies adjacent, forming either part of a crescent-shaped rampart that cut across the promontory or (more likely) the denuded vestiges of a ringwork, with suggestions that its ditch embraced the church. While the site has never been excavated, it stands out as a prime candidate for a thegnly residence with a dual purpose tower – part military (as a watchtower) and part religious (as a private chapel) – as the place was an important late Anglo-Saxon estate centre. Our sample of comparable sites is tiny, with fewer than thirty known examples of tower-nave churches of the period (Shapland 2008); countless others must have been demolished and/or remodelled and numerous examples – maybe hundreds – of thegnly residences must lie buried beneath Norman earth and timber castles.

Besides their poor survival rate as landscape features, one reason why such sites are so difficult to interpret, and the labels we might apply to them are uncertain – early manor houses? proto-castles? secular towers? – is that some familiar distinctions quickly break down. Once again, we are in the murky area between 'public' and 'private' defence: the Anglo-Saxon *burh-geat* was in essence a private home, but thegns emerged in the ninth century as high-status servants of the king, and their fortifications clearly aided the defence of the early English state. It cannot be coincidental that many known tower-churches stood near meeting places or mustering points, and/or on physically prominent sites that overlooked key communications routes including *herepaths* (military roads) and served as nodal points within networks of beacons. The architecture of thegnly towers once again blurs the division between 'secular' and 'ecclesiastical' architectural forms, and it is instructive that some of the most important new light shed on the origins of the castle in England has come from church archaeology.

While this debate about 'private' defence in late Anglo-Saxon England has largely concerned rural sites, archaeologists have identified potential equivalents in pre-Conquest towns, although admittedly in small numbers – sites such as St Michael at the Northgate, Oxford, which was the likely *burh-geat* of an urban aristocrat or official. Oxford contained at least one other comparable structure – the larger St George's tower, which stood by the west gate of the *burh* and was incorporated into the Norman castle. Both buildings feature characteristic upper-level doorways on their exteriors. Similar buildings in other towns have doubtless been swept away or re-built, with only the topographical positions of later churches or chapels suggesting origins as thegnly towers. In nearby Wallingford (Oxfordshire), for example, the Anglo-Saxon *burh* had six churches positioned on or near the defences, including one each on the east and west gates. These examples remind us once again that the image of the classic Anglo-Saxon royal *burh* as a 'communal' fortification can be misleading; they also accommodated the assets of elite stakeholders in late Saxon society and provided enclaves for the development and expression of private power.

Examining the exteriors of these late Anglo-Saxon churches, Derek Renn has drawn particular attention to the emblematic significance of doorway-like features in upper levels 'opening into space' in what are termed 'towers of display' (1994: 180-2). Whether they displayed people, relics or something else is moot; what is certain is that essentially similar architectural ideas found expression in early Norman towers within castles (Fig. 19). Exeter's gatehouse (*c.* 1070) is particularly intriguing given that the twin openings are Anglo-Saxon in style, perhaps even re-used from a church or chapel; more usually they were Romanesque in form, as at Bramber (West Sussex), Ludlow (Shropshire), Newark (Nottinghamshire), Richmond (North Yorkshire) and Sherborne (Dorset), which are all dated before *c.* 1150. In none of these cases were the openings militarily effective in any way; indeed they detracted from the sites' defensibility, being far too big for arrow loops and clearly not working as machicolations. This type of design follows no known French parallel or model, pointing to a synthesis of Anglo-Saxon traditions within early castle-building practices. It provides another salutary reminder that the castle was not exported wholesale from France as a fully finished product; the Conquest was a time of experimentation with fortification, which continued to evolve and metamorphose, drawing in part from an underestimated but extant heritage of lordly defence.

4. Nailing the Valley: Early Towers

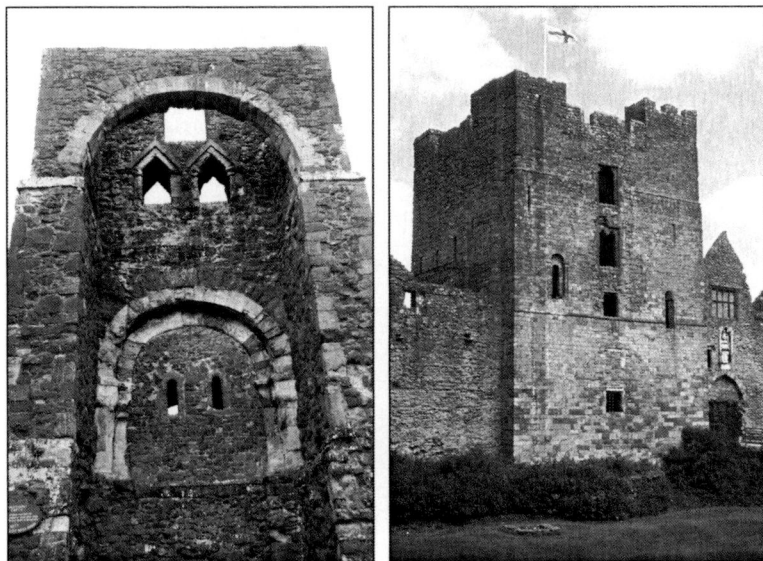

Fig. 19. Late eleventh-century gatehouses at Exeter (left) and Ludlow (right). Among the very earliest examples of masonry castle architecture in England, both structures preserve 'display' openings above the gate portal; Exeter preserves two triangular-headed features and Ludlow originally had a line of four in the Romanesque style, of which one survives.

Summary

The pre-eminent purpose of the great tower and the principal reason for its popularity in Europe was its value as a statement in stone of seigneurial power. These buildings were icons of status, authority and justice as well as projecting real and imagined military might. While our attention has inevitably been drawn towards the more major better-preserved examples, most donjons also had in common vertical hierarchies of planning and exerted a powerful visual impact on their surrounding territories and settlements. The builders of many donjons emulated Carolingian rulers by appropriating material heritage of the Roman past to fake historicity and bolster their positions. They were also hybrid buildings in many ways, bridging the gap between secular and ecclesiastical architecture and retaining a strong private character while making visual statements to wider populations, while larger examples were intended partly as arenas for public acts and ceremonies. The innovation of the great tower was not a technological one, but of integrating these seemingly contradictory roles within a single unified conception redolent with symbolism.

5

Early Castle Archaeologies: Themes and Debates

This chapter explores how archaeological investigation is deepening our understanding of Europe's 'castral revolution'. It is largely through large-scale multi-season archaeological excavation that our understanding of the plans and appearances of Europe's first castles has developed, and some of the greatest successes have unsurprisingly involved sites that were abandoned relatively early, their remains unencumbered by later development. A fuller picture has emerged as archaeologists lifted their initial gaze from defences, which characterised the approaches of the 1950s and 60s, to pay increasing attention to castle interiors and, more recently, their wider settings, although there has generally been insufficient emphasis on the social lives of early castles and their overall significance as cultural artefacts.

If there is a single lesson to be drawn from what is now a large array of thoroughly excavated early castle across Europe it is that surviving field monuments conceal highly individualistic sequences of occupation that cannot be predicted even vaguely from morphology alone. That the spatial planning and defences of these sites also invariably developed incrementally is reflected in a wide range of important excavations in addition to the key case studies on which this book focuses. Among the more prominent cases in point are investigations (in France) at Château Ganne (Calvados), Château-Thierry (Aisne), Montfélix (Marne) and Villars-les-Dombes (Ain); and (in Germany) at Burg Bommersheim (Hessen) and Elmendorf, Oldenburg (Lower Saxony).

The European timber castle?

The lingering preconception of the medieval castle as an edifice of stone is extraordinarily difficult to shake off. Yet archaeology is underlining as never before that in many contexts castles built mostly of earth and timber were not only the norm, especially between the eleventh and thirteenth centuries, but that these sites could embody the same sorts of symbolism – of lordship, authority and dominance – more generally associated with masonry fortifications.

Brian Hope-Taylor's excavations at Abinger (Surrey) in 1949 rightly attained classic status for the pioneering recovery of evidence for ephemeral timber structures on the motte top; his prioritisation of defensive features was characteristic of early investigations of earth and timber castles more generally (Higham and Barker 1992: 36-113, 293-6). It is unfortunate, however, that the famous reconstruction drawing of this motte-top structure – a watchtower rather than any sort of permanent building – became so influential in how archaeologists around Europe came to understand the physical appearances of earth and timber castles, partly because this phase of the site represented a temporary and martial work of the mid-twelfth century on the site of an earlier Norman seat of lordship, but also because wider open area excavations of equivalent sites have since afforded a very different image.

This is exemplified most famously by Hen Domen (Montgomeryshire), on the Anglo-Welsh border (Higham and Barker 2000). Excavation of the bailey interior shows a complex, bustling site built using sophisticated timber technologies, with an external appearance bristling with menace and power. The findings are influential: in Ireland, for instance, historians and archaeologists traditionally saw the 450 or so Anglo-Norman motte castles as impermanent military installations and poor relations to masonry fortifications; a newer view interprets them not only as altogether more permanent and seriously defended sites, but as busy manorial centres (O'Conor 2002).

We should remember that in the politically decentralised

world of the tenth and eleventh centuries it was individualism that members of the elite would have been anxious to express through the practice of castle building, and the archaeological record reflects this as well. Reviewing the rich evidence from Normandy, which is host to one of Europe's greatest concentrations of excavations on earth and timber castles – including sites such as Grimbosq, Mirville, Plessis-Grimoult and Bretoncelles – Flambard-Héricher (2002) comments that it is diversity of building practices and sequences across a relatively homogeneous geographical area that is the most remarkable characteristic of our data set. Across France as a whole, however, the understanding of bailey interiors still represents a notable lacuna in knowledge (Boucharlat 2009).

Against this background, two fundamental points are worthy of particular emphasis in our overall understanding and interpretation of earth and timber castles.

First, the medieval 'earthwork castle' simply never existed. While this term is still commonplace in archaeological writing it also deeply misleading as it neglects that the earthworks of early castles were nearly always built with the express purpose of supporting superstructures such as palisades or towers and to enclose other buildings that were very often also built of timber. Present-day landscapes of course preserve almost infinite varieties of castle earthwork, and the archaeologist's enduring predilection to slot these into neat typologies and schemes of classification, often specific to individual regions and countries, shows little sign of abating. To medieval contemporaries who saw and experienced these places, it would arguably have been the appearance of the timberwork that was most visually striking, with the form of related earthworks not always readily apparent and sometimes completely hidden from view. It was also arguably the quality and sophistication of timber superstructures that differentiated 'castles' from other forms of enclosed settlement or residence in the eyes of chroniclers – something that continued obsession with the earthwork vestiges of these sites completely neglects.

That said, we should also remember that the very distinction between castles of stone and castles of earth and timber is itself not always clear-cut, as several of the examples discussed in this chapter make clear. While the evidence is easily separated into these two categories, many early private fortifications took the form of masonry towers within earthwork enclosures topped with palisades, or of complexes of timber buildings encircled by stone walls. By the same token, virtually all stone castles incorporated some timber buildings of some sort so that a rigid distinction between these two technologies was again not always apparent in the medieval countryside.

The second important introductory point here is that we should not automatically assume that building a fortification in stone was necessarily a preferred option to constructing it in wood, or that timber castles were somehow inferior to masonry fortresses in terms of their appearance, social status and defensibility. In many parts of Europe including Germany, earth and timber fortifications have been seen as the domain of prehistorians, and have traditionally been afforded a low archaeological priority, with signs that this is changing only relatively recently. Possession of a masonry castle was not somehow a natural aspiration of all early castle-builders; indeed, in many contexts the perception of stone as a superior building material to wood is clearly the product of a post-medieval world view.

We should bear in mind the simple fact that the vast majority of sites that might loosely be termed early castles comprised complexes of earth and timber that were never re-built in stone. The explanation that this is because their lords lacked the resources is insufficient and again misrepresents the medieval mind-set; in numerous regions, especially those without readily available building stone, fortifications of earth and timber were the accepted practice, and builders were perfectly able to innovate within these parameters. It is important here that we treat critically any cosy evolutionary narrative of castle development during the period that involved, for instance, a widespread replacement of timber technologies with stone. Across great tracts of Europe, many thousand timber castles served as fortified estate centres in their own particular social and landscape contexts. While their construction used long-established technologies and resources marshalled from local networks, our growing body of excavated evidence makes it abundantly clear that timber castles too could constitute impressive displays of lordship and need not be dismissed as humble precursors to stone equivalents.

Timber castles: forms and locations

The total distribution of earth and timber castles between the ninth and eleventh centuries is unknown and – given the frequency with which their sites are lost and destroyed, both through agriculture and development and also because so many otherwise undocumented castles will have been perpetuated by later lordship sites – probably impossible to map. Yet it must comprise many tens of thousands of sites, stretching from areas of Scotland and Ireland characterised by distinctive Gaelic cultures and models of lordship, across huge swathes of north-western Europe, through to the Slavic lands in the east. In some senses the technology of the timber castle was ultimately inherited from prehistory, but there are other important and more immediate antecedents. The defences of Danish 'geometric fortresses' built in the late tenth century were similarly of earth and timber construction, although these were quite unlike castles in a functional and social sense, being garrisoned fortresses of the state that were unattached to estates or the workings of the land but part and parcel of a wider system of frontier defence and urban fortifications established by royal initiative. The construction and active use of timber fortifications in Europe also continued much later than is often acknowledged. In the Baltic states, for example, hillforts and promontory forts with timber defences were operational from the second half of the first millennium AD into the eleventh century and beyond, with many sites featuring prominently in the struggle with the Teutonic Order. Medieval Lithuania in particular has been characterised as a 'land of hillforts'; one

Fig. 20. Vihiers, showing a large *motte féodale* (motte) which may have been associated with an early fortification of Fulk Nerra.

estimate is that perhaps 60% of the thousand or more sites here were active at some time between the eleventh and fifteenth centuries (Zabiela 1996).

With the aforementioned caveats about the dangers of typologies in mind, there is no escaping the fact that earth and timber castles were built in two main ways: as mottes or as ringworks. Mottes (Fig. 20) were partially or fully artificial mounds that provided elevated positions for defensive or other high-status structures. As such, they had important psychological qualities, asserting an unmistakable lordly aura regardless of topographical setting, their very form proclaiming control over nature itself. The variations in morphology, chronology and associations are practically infinite, although a common view is that the 'classic' motte supported a central tower and had a bailey appended to it. In other cases, however, structures were sunk into mottes or were primary features around which mottes were raised (*emmottée* in French). Multiple mottes within single castral complexes are not unknown; clear examples in France known from excavation include double mottes at

5. Early Castle Archaeologies: Themes and Debates

Fig. 21. Duno: the earthworks of an early castle overlooking the Rhine near Arnhem; the site probably represents a ringwork fortification subsequently converted into a motte and bailey by heightening the southern end of the enclosure (bottom right of photograph).

Douai (Nord) and Montfélix (Marne), while in Germany the site of Burg Elmendorf (Ammerland) developed from a flatland settlement into a treble-mounded timber castle comprising two mottes and a raised bailey by the twelfth century.

Ringworks (Fig. 21) were ditched and embanked enclosures enclosing halls and other domestic buildings, their defences relying on the strength of the enclosing bank, palisade and gatehouse. The distinction between the two forms was blurred and fluid, however, and only partly because medieval builders created hybrid earthworks, as erosive post-abandonment processes have often reduced mottes and filled in ringworks. We should certainly remember that rigid distinctions of this kind, between earthworks with often subtly different morphologies, might be completely meaningless in medieval terms. Crucially, while the word 'motte' has medieval ancestry (giving rise to the Spanish *mota*, Italian *motta* and French and German *motte*), the term 'ringwork' is a piece of modern archaeological jargon. As a category of site it has a far wider chronological and geographical range than the motte and is less readily diagnostic of castle-building.

As well as offering an alternative to the motte in many Western European contexts, the ringwork fortress – *Ringwälle* in German – is well known from early medieval Central and Eastern Europe, although they do not equate neatly to 'castles'. The expansive site of Gniezno, in Poland, for instance, developed as a stronghold from the middle of the tenth century, possessing powerful ringwork defences built around a structure of enormous logs with layers of clay, sand and stone. Archaeologists in Germany and Poland long interpreted the small oval-shaped fortifications (often confusingly labelled as hillforts) that are found in large numbers in the lowlands as products of Slavic immigration and settlement in the late sixth and seventh centuries. Germany alone has well over one thousand such sites, although only a tiny proportion has received archaeological attention (Ettel 2008: 163). New dendrochronological dates for key sites have now established that this tradition of fortification dates to the late ninth and (especially) tenth centuries, with these compact ringforts replacing larger hill-top rampart enclosures and closely tied to the rise of a noble-like elite (Brather 2004: 321-3).

Mottes were built very widely within Europe: they are found from Ireland in the west to Poland and the Czech lands in the east, and from Denmark and Scotland in the north down to Sicily in the south, where the Normans moulded a small number from natural rocky eminences, although they are generally less common in the Mediterranean sphere. Mottes are also rare in Iberia, where stone remained the predominant technology of fortification. The idea of the motte was also never really exported to the Latin East during the Crusades, where there is little evidence for timber castles at all, with only one or two motte-like siege works known from documentary references. The European landscape of the tenth century as a whole was less densely scattered with mottes than previously thought; excavation and fieldwork is revealing increasing numbers of these features and showing that they clearly extended far down the scale, but archaeological dating (where available) is showing consistently that the heyday of their construction in many regions was the eleventh and twelfth centuries, as in Normandy and the Rhineland. To take a more detailed example: analysis of archaeological dating evidence for fifty mottes across Belgium and Holland shows that the phenomenon originated in the mid-eleventh century and reached its apogee in the twelfth, and that mottes continued to be built into the thirteenth century (De Meulemeester 1994). While medieval Norway had only a handful of castles, one of the earliest took the form of a motte, as revealed by excavations within the royal residence at Oslo, exposing a sand-built motte of *c.* 1050-60 encompassed by a moat (Ekroll 1998: 66).

It would certainly be a mistake to see mottes as diagnosably 'early' forms of castle building, however; in Denmark, Ireland and Scotland they were built into the late thirteenth and even the fourteenth centuries, but this was not restricted to Europe's supposed peripheries. In France archaeologists now accept that the early pattern of motte-building has been overestimated; as a form of construction the motte proclaimed the antiquity and legitimacy of noble lines, so that they were not only retained and curated but also constructed well into the thirteenth century (Renoux 2010: 241-43). In England too castle-builders were experimenting with the motte idea well into the heyday of masonry castle-building: Lydford, in Devon, preserves a 'false' motte, thrown up around a rebuilt masonry tower in the late thirteenth century, seemingly to evoke an antique image. Mottes were also built to impress as well as defend; at Goltho (Lincolnshire) the motte was studded with pebbles to give the impression from a distance of a stone tower, while at Hen Domen (Montgomery) timber superstructures were plastered and whitewashed to resemble stonework.

The physical locations that motte-builders chose were also incredibly varied. In northern Italy, for example, the scarped hilltop motte was a familiar landmark, while in Alpine France mottes are even found on precipitous peaks overlooking mountain passes (the example at Brandes, Isère, at 1840m has a claim to be the highest in Europe: Aarts 2007: 37). More typically, mottes nestled close to villages or other settlements, often adjacent to a church or chapel and maybe a fishpond, mill or dovecote. Inaccessible sites chosen purely for their defensibility are rarer than might be imagined; most were built on locations chosen for their viability as agricultural and administrative centres and their visibility to populations. In Holland, meanwhile, many hundreds of lordly mottes were constructed as elements within wetland reclamation schemes in low-lying zones, as witnessed in areas such as Friesland and Zeeland in the eleventh and especially the twelfth centuries, although the much earlier tradition of building *terpen* or *wierden* (raised habitation sites) creates potential for confusion and in some cases blurs with motte construction.

New archaeological discoveries can prompt rapid re-assessment. A remarkable multi-method field analysis by the Laboratory for Landscape Archaeology and Remote Sensing at the University of Siena of a site first recognised through aerial photography in 2005 has revealed the first earth and timber castle in Tuscany – a region well known for its numerous early *roccas* (hilltop seigneurial towers), but where mottes were entirely unknown. Known as Castellina, near the better known castle of Scarlino on the Tuscan coastal plain, the site was investigated through three different methods of geophysical prospection as well as field-walking and trail excavation, confirming the presence of a triple-ditched enclosure around a denuded mound that may mantle a central building (Fig. 22); the complex covered an area of around one hectare and was dated to the eighth to ninth century AD (Campana et al. 2009). This discovery is of considerable interest given that the high intensity of fieldwork in the region more generally had not previously indicated comparable sites, largely as their archaeological signatures are not readily visible through field-walking. It reminds us of the wider problem that archaeologists sometimes have prescribed views of the morphological

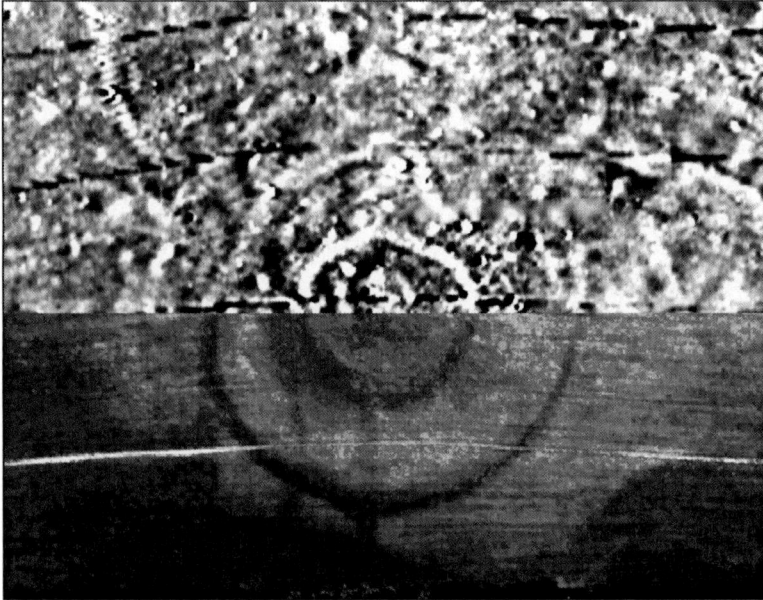

Fig. 22. Geophysical survey and aerial photograph of the remains of an early earth and timber castle at the site of Castellina in Tuscany.

forms that early castles should take, so that sites which do not fit a supposed norm are potentially overlooked.

Excavation of early castles: challenges and lessons

Despite the different technologies employed in early castle construction, the essential spatial ordering of activities has sufficient in common for us to contemplate an underlying 'grammar' of internal planning. The problem is that this has been obscured by the variety of external forms – in particular defences – on which so much archaeological effort has concentrated. As has been established, more or less universal to the spatial planning of early castles was their sub-division into units graded according to social status and the fact that while their overall plans were curved and/or irregular, the structures within were rectangular. In short, they appeared exotic from the outside but familiar from the inside. The *Castrum* d'An-done (Charente), in the Charente *département* of central-west-ern France provides us with a particularly illustrative case in point (Bourgeois 2009). This seat of the Counts of Angoulême was constructed in the second half of the tenth century but abandoned by *c.* 1020, and its structure, development and material culture have been revealed in exceptionally fine detail through excavations over a quarter of a century directed by André Debord. The compact *castrum* was replaced by a much larger fortification at nearby Montignac, on the banks of the Charente, perhaps because it was too small to house a popula-tion of *milites* or soldiers owing service.

At Andone we have a site undisturbed by later occupation, providing a window into the social and economic life of a castle at a pivotal period in their emergence. The site comprises an oval masonry circuit embracing a series of stone-built 'lean-to' structures (Fig. 23). Despite the irregular plan and crowded interior, this internal arrangement followed a clear spatial logic, being divided into three zones of buildings each with an associated open space. The formal east entrance opened into a private courtyard where the principal hall stood over a lower hall; an intermediate zone, screened from view, focused on private *camerae* or chambers with latrines; and a large service zone occupied the western area. Provision of two separate en-trances gave further structure to this early 'bi-polar' plan, encompassing a modest area of only 2000m^2 which is broadly comparable to other fortified courts of the late tenth and early eleventh centuries, including Boves (Somme), Langoiran (Gi-ronde), Montsoreau (Maine et Loire) and (in Germany) the palace of Broich, near Mülheim an der Ruhr (Bourgeois 2009: 450-9).

Of these, the spur-top site of Boves, near Amiens, deserves comment for the especially detailed archaeological attention it has received, showing how its lords transformed an *oppidum* into a medieval castle (Racinet 2010). An enormous platform, 12m high, 50m across and involving the movement of perhaps 45,000m^3 of material, was added to the pre-existing rampart;

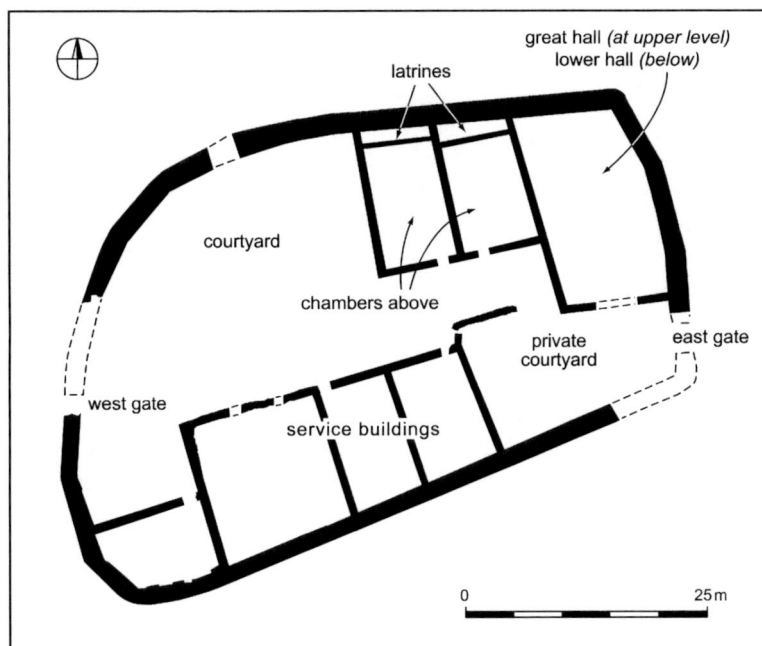

Fig. 23. *Castrum* d'Andone: plan of the excavated site.

radiocarbon dating of deposits within it and thermoluminescence dating of tiles from buildings upon it mean that we can
attribute this prodigious development to the early tenth century. The exceptional survival of around two metres of
stratigraphy preserved successive phases of occupation
marked by the zoning of robust lordly buildings with industrial
and agricultural areas, with other direct evidence of a high-
status presence apparent in the finds assemblage, including
pearl rings and, quite exceptionally, crucibles showing that
gold was smelted under the seigneurial gaze.

Another very clear example of the transformative potential
of large-scale excavation to shed new light not only on the
structures but also the social lives of early castles is Sugny
castle (or Tchesté de la Rotche: 'the castle on the rock') (Fig. 24).
Excavations initiated by the Belgian Archaeological Service

97

from the 1980s afford us a glimpse into a castle that was also a pioneer settlement, probably founded by the counts of Bouillon and buried deep in the densely forested Belgian Ardennes (Matthys 1991). Crucially, the key phases of early castle growth were again not obscured by later development, with occupation ceasing by the beginning of the twelfth century. The site shows well how the technologies and forms of early castles are not always easily classifiable: although it has the appearance of a motte, it was scarped from a pedestal of living rock, into which post-holes for a timber superstructure were cut. From possible Carolingian origins, the site was re-planned in the late tenth or early eleventh century around a square wooden tower around nine metres across, supported by squared corner posts up to *c.* 85cm thick, and with a cellar below; ancillary timber buildings included a kitchen that lay within a palisaded enclosure on a slightly lower plateau. The tower's replacement in stone before *c.* 1100 coincided with an intensification of craft-working activity indicated by a miscellany of workshops on the lower area but also a tighter and more hierarchical zoning of the site through the cutting of a large rock-cut ditch between the hilltop and the plateau. This defined an upper bailey which, while accessible from the lower bailey, provided no route of circulation with the donjon, which formed an independent unit; a clear differentiation of status is also apparent in the remarkable animal bone assemblage (pp. 115-16).

These aforementioned sites are archaeologically atypical in some way, because their lords abandoned them early, because of remarkable conditions of stratigraphic preservation, or both. Salutary lessons on the potential limitations of archaeological evidence for early castles are provided by the Royal Archaeological Institute's project *The Origins of the Castle in England*, established in 1966 to mark the 900th anniversary of the Norman Conquest of England (Davison 1967). A bold attempt to engage with the then contentious topic of castle origins through allied historical and archaeological research, the project combined fieldwork in Normandy with five flagship excavations of

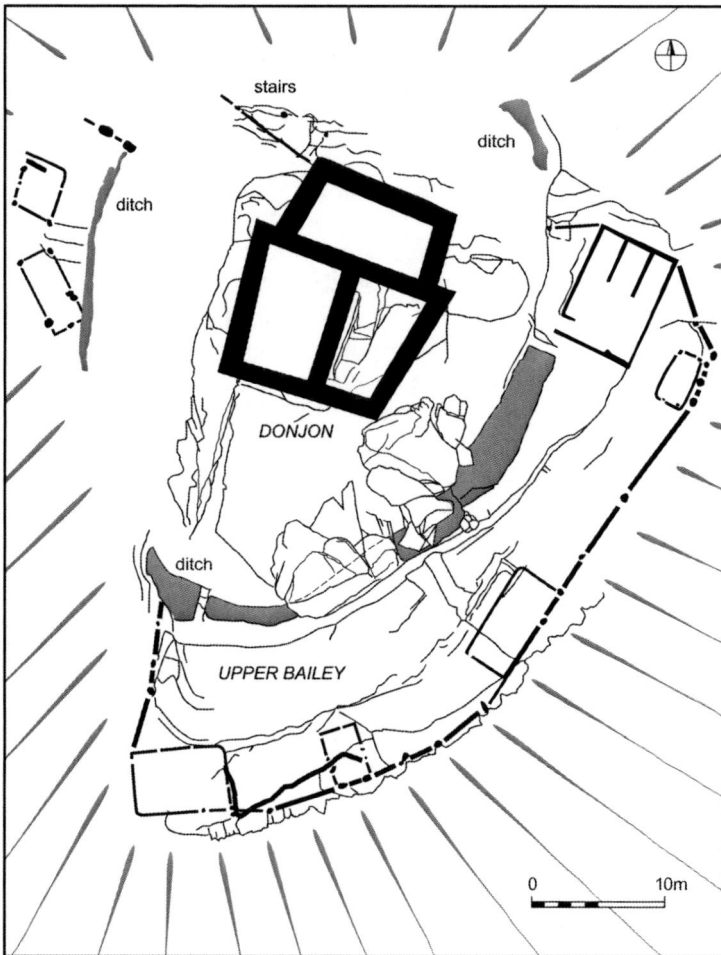

Fig. 24. Plan of the castle of Sugny (or Tchesté de la Rotche: 'the castle on the rock').

sites in England (Baile Hill in York; Bramber, West Sussex; Hastings, East Sussex; Hen Domen, Montgomeryshire; and Sulgrave, Northamptonshire). Evaluating the project, Saunders (1977: 5) judged that it had 'raised more questions than it has solved'. While representing a rare case of a co-ordinated attempt to answer specific questions through a multi-faceted research strategy, the very varied successes of the excavations highlight key methodological problems associated with the excavation of early earth and timber castles. Most notably, the physical traces of these sites can be fragile in the extreme, being prone to destruction by later phases of occupation and erosion, so that evidence of date and the nature of occupation can be inconclusive. Perhaps most importantly, however, the project showed in particularly sharp focus that archaeological evidence is, by its very nature, not at its most effective when used to answer what are essentially historical questions.

Experiences across Europe tell us that early phases of castle growth can prove extraordinarily difficult to date. Two examples of well known and frequently cited excavations where early dates for private fortifications have been challenged show the extent of the problem. At Goltho, in Lincolnshire (England) a sequence of aristocratic occupation began in the late Saxon period with a timber hall embraced within a defensive earthwork enclosure (dated to *c.* 850 but later enlarged) and culminated in a castle site, first of motte and bailey form (*c.* 1080), and finally a hall surmounting a raised platform created by filling in the bailey (*c.* 1150) (Beresford 1987). Details of the re-evaluation are complex, but essentially the excavator probably paid insufficient attention to the pottery and finds assemblage and placed too much reliance on spurious historical reasoning in dating the first ringwork enclosure; the result is that the entire phasing needs to be pushed forwards in time, by perhaps fifty years (Hodges 1988). This might appear a minor detail, as it doesn't alter the fact that a gated and seriously defended lordly compound existed here well over a century before 1066; more important perhaps is that fact that the motte phase can now be dated several generations later than the Norman Conquest (perhaps to the 'Anarchy' period, *c.* 1140-50). The implication is important: the archaeological signature of the Norman Conquest was not as profound as originally thought, with a local noble inhabiting a ringwork-style fortification adjacent to his estate church and lording it over the peasantry in more or less the same style either side of this supposed historical watershed.

Comparable in some ways is the site of der Husterknupp, located north-west of Cologne in the German Rhineland. Adolf Herrnbrodt's classic excavations here similarly showed a motte and bailey castle to have been preceded by several earlier phases of enclosed settlement, here in the context of a low-lying site with waterlogged conditions making for the outstanding archaeological survival of timber structures. From late ninth-century origins claimed by the excavator the site's defences were progressively elaborated and its spatial planning increasingly defined; this saw a palisaded and moated flatland settlement sub-divided into two zones, with an upper part elevated on a low earthwork platform. The site developed into a powerfully defended motte and bailey between the eleventh and thirteenth centuries, the *Hochmotte* (high motte) standing over 6m high, although details of its superstructure were not recovered (Herrnbrodt 1958). Yet revised dating of the site's ceramic sequence means that the earliest phase seems to date to the mid-tenth century (Friedrich 1994). Again, the entire sequence can be pushed forwards in time. This also prompts us to question the excavator's interpretation that the defensive developments represented a response to Viking threats, with internal social change and a gradual ramping up of lordly power seeming a viable alternative.

The distinction between estate centres and castles in the period is blurred. Excavations are revealing ever increasing numbers of long-term sequences of castle 'evolution' whereby fortified seigneurial centres emerged gradually from manorial origins. Petegem, in Flanders, Belgium, is one of our clearest examples (Loveluck 2005: 237-8). Here an eighth-century timber-built elite compound centred on a hall and church was upgraded in the ninth century through rebuilding in stone and by the cutting of a ditch, seven metres wide, that created a bipartite plan resembling a figure of eight. The site subsequently developed into what was unambiguously a castle although in its earlier phase the 'defences' served to define and differentiate this important estate centre and meeting place rather than to serve a military purpose.

The traditional view that fortifications were somehow out of the ordinary in Carolingian society cannot therefore be sustained; nor can the notion that its rulers were hard on the builders of private defences. In some cases the 'origin point' of a castle comprised little more than a cosmetic makeover for an extant seat of lordship. The body of supporting archaeological evidence is growing rapidly; mottes were demonstrably secondary additions to extant lordly complexes at sites such as Mellier in Belgium, the Tour d'Albon (Drôme, France). Another illustrative case in point is the earth and timber castle known as 'Hoge Andjoen' at Werken (West Flanders, Belgium), a site outwardly classifiable as a motte and bailey preceded by a moated Carolingian *Flachsiedlung* ('flat settlement') (Van Strydonck and Vanthournout 1996). Here, the motte, which reached 6m in height and 50m in diameter, was of at least eight separate construction phases (AD 860-960), comprising successive elevations above the floodplain, of greater and lesser scale and occurring at uneven intervals, which preserved excellent occupation layers. Such was the nature of the build-up that it is difficult to define at which point the site actually became a motte, and it is impossible to differentiate flood-prevention, defence and the projection of status as potential driving forces behind the construction.

Case studies from Ireland and Holland / Germany

Two case studies of apparently prodigious early traditions of castle building in contrasting parts of Europe – the area of the Lower Rhine on the present Dutch/German border and the west of Ireland – allow us to home in on several of the aforementioned issues in more detail.

A critical theme in the debate over the origins of timber castles is that early writers are inconsistent and – to our minds – imprecise and even confused in the terminology they used to describe lordly fortifications. This in many ways parallels a similar issue in our understanding of early masonry towers (p. 71). An enlightening source that brings this issue into sharp focus is the *De diversitate temporum* of Alpert of Metz, *c.* 1023-4, which provides an account of a power struggle amongst the lords of the Lower Rhine in which timber castles feature prominently, being built to make claims on the land and frequently attacked by rivals. To take one example: Alpert talks of a *castellum* constructed for Count Wichman of Vreden around 1011; it was apparently formed from a small hill within an inaccessible marsh linked to the River Meuse and incorporated towers and a *vallum* (an earthwork bank), making it quite unclear as to whether this equates to a motte, a ringwork or something else (Aarts 1996: 13). The site is now lost, making any correlation with physical remains impossible. What is particularly important here is the deliberate reference to the site being built in the style of *studenti novis rebus* ('anyone eager for a change') – medieval code for something revolutionary (Bartlett 1993: 68). In this snapshot account timber castles were clearly not unknown but represented something experimental and novel, and visibly so.

A relevant structure known in detail through archaeology is Montferland in the Netherlands (Fig. 25). J.G.N. Renaud excavated the site in the 1960s and it has been re-interpreted by Schut (2003), who identifies it as the early eleventh-century stronghold of Opladen, mentioned by Alpert of Metz for its extraordinary stone walls. Many things about the site do not fit into a 'standard' model of a motte. For a start, the mound is unusually large, up to *c.* 20m high, and although it was built on a natural hill, construction is estimated to have involved moving 95,000m^3 of earth, making it the largest motte in the Netherlands and one of the largest anywhere in north-west Europe. A curtain wall circumscribed a large level platform that contained a substantial hall at one end and a square stone tower built of re-used Roman 'tufa' at the other. Here, as elsewhere, the dichotomy between fortifications of stone and timber breaks down – and that is not all: the site is part-motte and part-ringwork. The arrangement does not fit into any category, pointing to its experimental character: the motte-top occupation area sees a hall and tower adjacent to one another when we would conventionally expect to find the latter in a bailey. The site was clearly more complex than this, with earthwork remains of at least one associated enclosure as well as concentric earthwork defences, which await detailed investigation.

The early eleventh century was clearly a period of experimentation with early castle forms, and the socio-political conditions around the Lower Rhine created a hotbed for it. Extensive fieldwork by Bas Aarts shows that sites of the period more generally sometimes took the form of a 'motte barrage' (where the motte is not separated from the bailey with a ditch, but joined to it), a 'motte *avancée*' (positioned as an outpost of the main complex) as well as the motte/ringwork (2007: 44-54). It is important that such features are not dismissed as anomalies or atypical forms, as almost infinite variation existed beyond the supposedly classical motte and bailey plan. Equally, however, we should remember that it was the appearance of timber defences rather than the earthworks that were remarkable to contemporaries, and we should be careful not to see field monuments such as these as rigid classes of prototype in a neat evolutionary sequence.

This question of antecedents to castle-building is especially relevant in Ireland, where the debate is particularly complex given the multiplicity of defended homesteads that dotted the early medieval rural landscape; these included raths/ring-forts (enclosed with earthen ramparts and ditches), cashels (protected by stone walls), and crannogs (in marshes and lakes) (O'Conor 1998: 73-94). Of the tens of thousands of such sites across Ireland, some were re-built as motte or ringwork castles in the wake of the Norman Conquest and colonisation after 1169. The lack of excavated examples means that interpretation is beset with problems, with identification of 'pre' and 'post' Conquest forms of construction extremely contentious. Again, however, mottes did not arrive into the landscape as entirely alien forms of construction, as some so-called 'raised raths' in Ulster have been shown to be entirely pre-Norman,

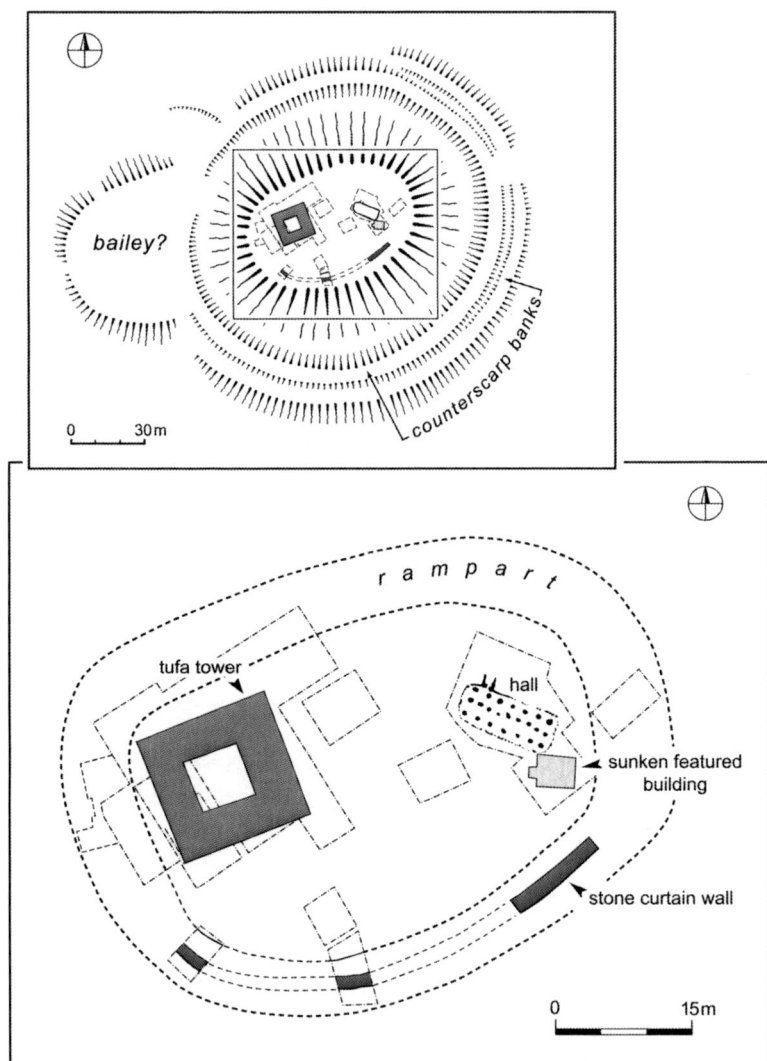

Fig. 25. Montferland: plan of the early castle, showing excavated features.

representing part of a tradition of what was essentially private defence that extended far back into the early medieval centuries.

The castle-like attributes of a group of eleventh- and twelfth-century fortifications in pre-Norman Connacht, in western Ireland, have been the subject of a particularly important debate and constitute a second case study. Sites such as Caislen na Caillighe (Co. Mayo), Iniscremha Island (Co. Galway) and the Rock of Lough Cé (Co. Roscommon) represent a tradition of what are sometimes termed 'super-cashels' characteristic of the region in the tenth and, in particular, the early eleventh centuries and built by Gaelic lords such as the O'Conor family (O'Conor et al. 2010). These were stone-walled fortifications, typically built on partly artificial islands within lakes and thus on sites with excellent visibility; architecturally they were distinguished by mortared walls and perhaps breastworks, but lacking the defensive and symbolic qualities that Anglo-Norman chroniclers associated with castles. From an archaeological point of view, these sites lacked the internal complexity and hierarchical sub-division that were hallmarks of castle planning (Fig. 26).

These new interpretations on the basis of fresh fieldwork indicate not only that their builders were drawing on long-established traditions of private defence (although realised on a larger scale), but that internal social change was the motor that accelerated investment by elites in stone fortifications, with Ireland moving towards a centralised monarchy by the twelfth century. This makes for a more convincing model than native rulers half heartedly buying into mainstream European notions of lordly display as they felt the first ripples of feudalisation.

Likewise, across swathes of Gaelic Ireland, Scotland and in parts of Wales, we should remember that lordship in kin-based societies was expressed in different ways to the supposed European 'norm'. In Scotland, for example, it is instructive that of 71 thanages (areas of land held by agents of the king, recorded from the twelfth century but originating earlier) only ten contain mottes, showing that these fortifications actually avoided

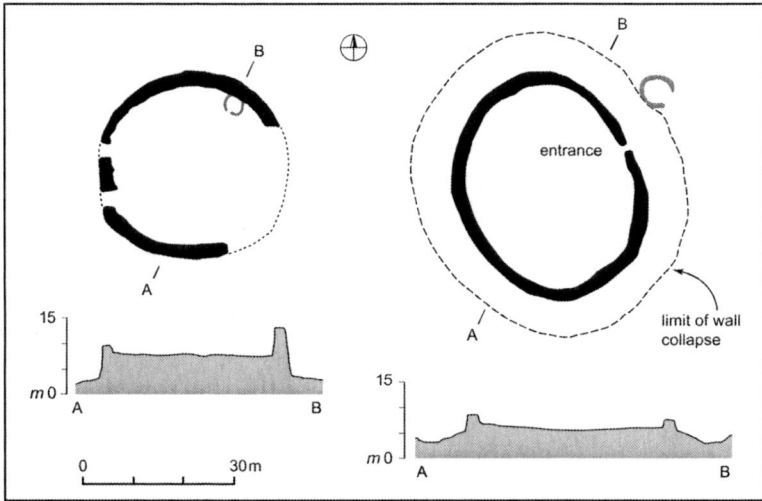

Fig. 26. Caislen na Caillighe (left) and Iniscremha (right): examples of eleventh- or twelfth-century 'super-cashels' in the west of Ireland.

old centres of power (Driscoll 1998). A marked lack of excavated sites means that we have even less idea of what the estate centres of the pre-Norman nobility looked like, but analogy with sites excavated in England is unlikely to be helpful given the distinctive Gaelic personality of lordship (Oram 2008: 170-1).

Summary

Earth and timber castles need no longer slot into the traditional 'castle story' as inferior antecedents and their construction technologies should not deflect from understanding these installations as icons of lordship in their own contexts. While earthwork and timber castles have sometimes been seen as a phenomenon that originated in northern France and spread to England and other parts of Europe from the eleventh century, a newer view sees indigenous early medieval societies as developing their own independent traditions of private defence that evolved within distinctive social environments, often gradu-

ally, into castle building. Another important shift in our thinking is that the morphological categories established by earlier
researchers are not waterproof, with distinctions between, for
example, earth and timber/stone castles and mottes/ringworks
mutable rather than fixed and in some cases artificial or totally
meaningless. Lacunae in the archaeology of early castles remain,
however: there has been too much concentration on defences
and too little on domestic arrangements and the social archaeology of these households.

6

Theatres of Lordship: Noble Lifestyles

The French expression *l'habitat aristocratique* ('aristocratic habitat') provides a helpful starting point that urges us to consider the social environments of early castles as distinct from their roles as fortifications. This chapter considers three aspects of everyday life within these sites: the portable material culture that excavations have produced and what this tells us about the new aristocracy; the roles of animals in noble culture as indicated by excavated bone assemblages; and the visual experiences of early castles from within and without.

Artefacts: seigneurial material culture?

An unfortunate tradition within the publication of many castle excavations is the relegation of finds reports to unappealing appendices lost at the backs of monographs, with results not always integrated into overall narratives in the way they deserve. The portable material culture recovered from early castles and other aristocratic sites is a subject in its own right, but a few salient observations are pertinent here and the topic as a whole deserves our closer scrutiny. The evidence ranges from more mundane objects to the highly unusual, with unambiguous evidence for an aristocratic presence often limited to a very small number of artefacts – most obviously personal adornments. The unfailing presence of agricultural tools tells us much about the humdrum everyday lives of these sites as farms. What is also consistent is the quite limited presence of diagnosably military artefacts; arrow-heads are the most common, although hunting forms are always mixed with military points, and finds of armour and weaponry (as distinct from tools) rare indeed. It is also through portable objects that we can detect the female presence within early castle communities – through certain dress accessories and objects associated with textile craftworking such as thimbles – as gender-specific domestic provision only really becomes apparent in later castle planning.

Many of these issues are borne out by the classic example of Hen Domen (Montgomeryshire, Wales), excavated between 1960 and 1992 and probably the most thoroughly investigated timber castle in Europe. The excavators revised their view of the character of daily castle life during the late eleventh- to thirteenth-century period of occupation from an initial image of a simple and hardy lifestyle, with little in the assemblage that pointed definitively to aristocratic occupation, to a more nuanced interpretation that high-status lifestyle is evident in the material culture, but in more subtle ways (Higham and Barker 2000: 173-80). This is partly a reflection of the pace with which these data were accumulated and analysed in a long-term project, with different categories of evidence sometimes pointing in different directions. Thus, while the range of pottery from Hen Domen is no different to that from any contemporary urban or rural site in the region, the animal bone bears the aristocratic hallmark of a preponderance of pigs. The array of metalwork is dominated by simple and utilitarian items but also contains some military finds (spurs, arrowheads and chain mail links) as well as gilded buckles and other personal effects.

A related research area with particular potential is the comparative analysis of finds from fortified centres and nearby communities, which can help us to engage with questions of social differentiation between lords and communities and, by extension, the mental construction of 'seigneurial' and 'settlement' space. Detailed comparison of a group of Swedish sites shows that the differences in personal material culture were far less marked than might be expected, with the overall quality of items comparing to equivalent sites elsewhere in Europe,

6. Theatres of Lordship: Noble Lifestyles

despite their supposedly peripheral context (Svensson 2008: 327-38). Among the more important distinguishers of noble identity were heraldic mounts and certain types of jewellery, including centuries-old heirlooms, testifying to complex negotiation with the past to express noble lineage.

Two brief case studies – of an especially important excavated site and a particularly illuminating type of find – allow some of these issues to be considered in a little more detail.

An especially informative site in this context is the *Castrum* d'Andone, which affords an exceptional snapshot of élite lifestyle in the late tenth and early eleventh centuries through a rich and massive finds assemblage (*c*. 116,000 separate objects). This captures perhaps better than any site in Europe the everyday activities of an elite household and their interaction with a wider castral community at a particularly important moment in the castle story. Striking is the correlation between the material culture of privilege and the highest status zone of the site in terms of domestic planning. The area of the hall and chambers is where finds of ceramic and stone lamps, gaming pieces, cabinet fittings, items relating to textile crafts (perhaps indicating a female presence) and glass from drinking vessels, windows and personal adornments are concentrated. This zone is also where proportions of venison are highest in the animal bone assemblage and glazed wares in the ceramics; still more exceptional finds included fragments of bone hunting horns, scales of armour plate, a bone flute, an exquisite enamelled brooch depicting a bird, and a single fragment of 'siliceous ware' derived from somewhere in the Middle East – perhaps Egypt or Turkey. Social division is apparent in the evidence that elsewhere in the complex others smelted metals, forged weapons and worked antler into items such as crossbow components. Particularly characteristic of the lower-status western zone of the site was the presence of equids (82% of iron objects from the site were related fittings, shoes and nails), while cattle are testified by cowbells. Other artefacts were more evenly distributed, including arrow heads (191 examples), coinage (20) and keys (115). The total package of seigneurial material culture is thus quite nuanced and extends beyond exceptional, rare and imported objects to include quantitative as well as qualitative indicators (Bourgeois 2009: 462-506).

A perhaps less than immediately obvious reflection of the Europeanisation of elite culture in the period of early castle building is the evidence in finds assemblages of common leisure pursuits. Finds of individual gaming pieces are not uncommon in excavations of early castles; carved from bone, ivory or antler, they derive from medieval forms of chess or *tabulae* (a form of backgammon), and examples have been found at many of the key sites discussed in this book, including Trim in Ireland and Colletière, Pineuilh and *Castrum* d'Andone in France (the latter with particularly large numbers recovered from beneath the great hall). These games are quite different from 'mereles' (or nine men's morris), for which evidence survives in the form of carved boards – a remarkable example from the early castle at Niozelles in Provence was inscribed on a stone re-used from a Neolithic context (Mouton 2008: 53). Most famous of all, the Lewis chessmen, dating from the twelfth to thirteenth centuries (and found in a hoard rather than a domestic context), are usually seen as the stock of a merchant when they were more probably the treasured possessions of a noble (Caldwell et al. 2009: 176). Board games might seem a fringe aspect of aristocratic culture, but they are worth considering in a little more detail as extremely rare forms of Romanesque art intended for secular audiences that provide an invaluable window into the self-image of the noble classes.

Tabulae boards and gaming sets of the period are particularly illustrative of this point as, of the three well attested examples from Western Europe, two (from Mayenne in northwest France and Gloucester, on the border between England and Wales) come from early castle contexts. The other instance (from Saint-Denis, in France) is from an early twelfth-century domestic cesspit and comprised a board without pieces. The eleventh- to twelfth-century assemblage from Mayenne (Fig. 27) consists of pieces from two separate chess sets and two or three *tabulae* sets, some of them unfinished, suggesting manu-

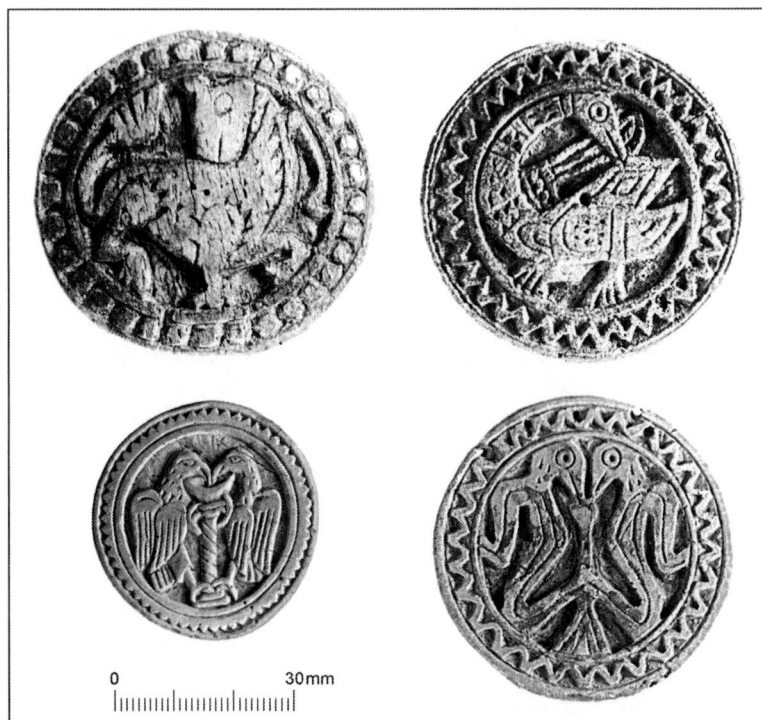

Fig. 27. Eleventh-/twelfth-century tablesmen from Mayenne.

facture within the castle, with others more likely imported from elsewhere, along with dice and the bone points formerly inlaid into a wooden board. Especially elaborate in design, the 23 circular counters or 'tablesmen' were characterised by carved zoomorphic and bird motifs with ring and dot decoration around the edges (Diez et al. 1998: 56-8).

The early twelfth-century set from the Norman castle in Gloucester comprised a full set of 30 counters carved from red deer bone and antler (perhaps significantly, given the allusions to hunting on their designs), along with a nearly complete board with ox rib panels, all found within a domestic pit (Darvill 1988: 31-2). It is worth pausing to consider quite how intimately this sort of evidence allows us to tap into a sense of elite identity in the period. Such was the value of *tabulae* sets that they must have been commissioned for noble patrons on an individual basis, their designs reflecting individual wishes. The elite passion for these games tells us about a love of gambling and a particularly intimate form of socialisation. Their designs, meanwhile, bring us as close to aristocratic lifestyle as we could reasonably hope to get. Individually crafted to reflect different facets of the aristocratic self-image, these were dominated by depictions of hunting, hawking and beasts of the chase, as well as images of feasting and drinking; music (a harpist) and other forms of courtly entertainment (a juggler).

Aristocratic diet and the ecology of early lordship

Before the evidence of recipe books, which become available from the thirteenth and fourteenth centuries onwards, archaeozoology (the archaeological study of animal bones) is our key source of evidence for the reconstruction of medieval elite diet, and we have the benefit of many hundreds of minutely analysed and often well-dated assemblages that, cumulatively, highlight some common traits. Of the more common species from medieval domestic sites – cattle, sheep and pig – it is the relatively high frequency of pig bones (sometimes exceeding 50%) that is the diagnostic signature of aristocratic occupation (Fig. 28). The consumption of pork is a key marker of social status in the early castle-building period, and the relatively young age of these animals when slaughtered (so as to obtain the meat at its juicy best) another. At the *Castrum* d'Andone, for example, the late tenth- and early eleventh-century animal bone assemblage comprised over 66% pig bones, as well as producing evidence for the exploitation of 29 species of wild bird and ten species of wild mammal, with the castle household apparently eating small quantities of squirrel, rabbit and hedgehog as well as sturgeon, heron and peacock (Bourgeois 2009: 323, 504-5).

6. *Theatres of Lordship: Noble Lifestyles*

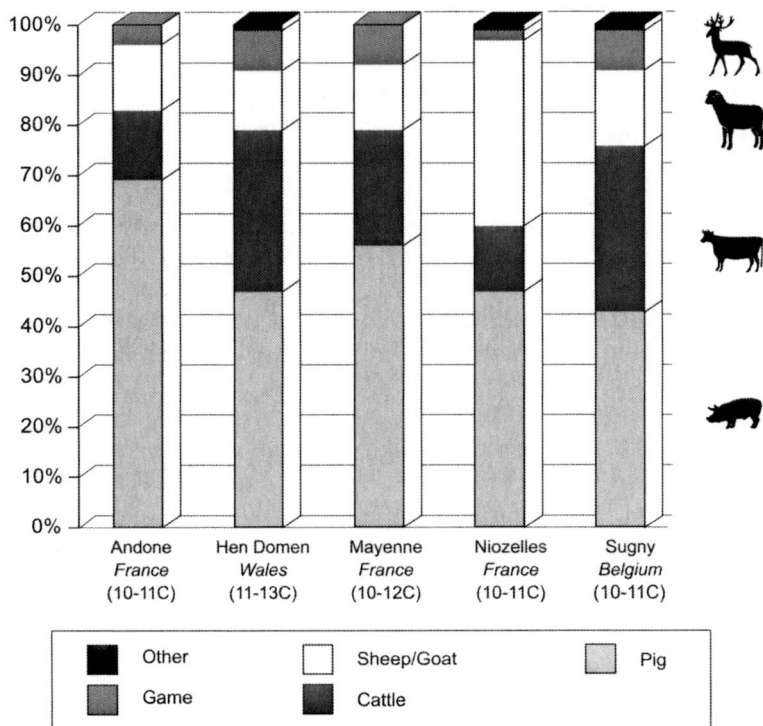

Fig. 28. Graph showing proportions of main types of mammal species from five early castle sites. The figures are for numbers of identifiable specimens (NISP) and the sample sizes are Andone (28,190), Hen Domen (1,160), Mayenne (4,899), Niozelles (18,476), and Sugny (2,886).

This presence of a wide variety of such wild hunted species is a further characteristic of early castle archaeozoology, as hunting was a socially restricted activity. Venison in particular clearly had international currency as the quintessential noble foodstuff; evidence for its consumption at fortified seigneurial sites of the tenth and eleventh centuries is widespread, in some cases showing that certain cuts – in particular haunches – were favoured. For example, the presence of roebuck is a consistent feature of the archaeozoological signatures of the first stone-built castles in the landscapes of Tuscany and Liguria as they emerged from villages in the tenth and eleventh centuries (Valenti and Salvatori 2008: 185-6). The other key hunted species were hare, fox, badger and wild boar, while even brown bear found its way onto the aristocratic table, as borne out by evidence from early castles in Belgium (Ervynck 2004: 216). There are good reasons to think that this change in the composition of animal bone assemblages – reflecting noble tastes – is essentially a pan-European phenomenon: excavations of Slavic strongholds from the ninth to twelfth centuries, for example, also consistently show the hunting and consumption of bird species and rare types of wild animal, especially boar (Brachmann 1983: 92-3).

The castle of Sugny (Belgium) (Fig. 29) provides an illuminating example. The presence of wild mammals (especially red deer but also hare, red squirrel, fox, roe deer and wild boar) again characterises the archaeozoology of this small hilltop castle of the tenth and eleventh centuries built as a 'pioneer' aristocratic settlement in a heavily forested zone. It is domestic species, however, that account for the vast majority of the overall bone assemblage, which charts wider ecological changes accompanying the seigneurial presence, including deforestation as cattle farming grew at the expense of pig herding (Ervynck and Woollett 2006). While the presence of diverse wild species is certainly diagnostic of aristocratic occupation the proportion of these animal bones is typically well under 10% on early castle sites (Fig. 29). Although their exploitation was essential to the aristocratic ecological imprint, wild creatures constituted a tiny proportion of overall aristocratic diet, and Sugny's lords clearly hunted for pleasure rather than for subsistence.

Also important here is evidence for the introduction of new species closely associated with aristocratic lifestyle. The spread of the rabbit across Western Europe from the Iberian Peninsula and southern France in the eleventh and twelfth centuries is intimately related to its exploitation by the nobility through artificial warrens, with castle sites supplying some of the earli-

6. Theatres of Lordship: Noble Lifestyles

Fig. 29. Sugny: view of the rock-cut motte.

est rabbit bones in different regions. More controversial is the case of fallow deer, which new studies show were probably introduced to England and northern France from the Mediterranean sphere through Norman connections with Sicily; again, much of the earliest evidence comes from castles, including cases where captured beasts were imported for display purposes, as with an enormous male specimen from Trowbridge castle (Wiltshire) which seems to be a first generation import – perhaps from Turkey or Greece (Sykes and Carden 2011: 149-50). The evidence of bird bones, meanwhile, confirms that aristocratic culture put a premium on the variety of species available for the aristocratic table, especially those from watery habitats (swan, heron, crane, which grew in popularity) and showpiece specimens such as peacock. For example, the first peacock bone in England is from Carisbrooke castle (Isle of Wight, England), dating from the late eleventh or early twelfth century (Serjeantson 2006: 142). In a rather different category are rare and exotic species ranging from elephants and lions to polar bears that were exchanged as gifts and sometimes maintained at the more important courts of

Europe, drawing on the notion of the Roman *vivaria* (Creighton 2009: 101-2).

The rich potential of castle archaeology to shed light on the seigneurial impact on landscapes in its totality is highlighted by the sort of integrated analysis carried out at Lanzenkirchen castle in Lower Austria, a twelfth- to fourteenth-century fortification of the lower nobility (Kühtreiber 1999). Extensive bioarchaeological sampling from layers within the bailey and its ditch unveil the agricultural opening of the site's environs; the usual aristocratic tastes are evident in the high proportion of pigs (mainly one or two years old) and the range of hunted species (here including alpine snow grouse alongside more familiar game); cereal production included buckwheat, showing potential Eastern European influences, and other lines of evidence confirm the presence of fishponds, gardens and a milling facility integrated into the site's moated defences.

Two points are particularly important here. First, the widespread ecological changes that accompanied early castles bear a remarkable level of pan-European comparison, which is remarkable given the geographical differences in the areas over which these sites are found. Such are the commonalities in the ecological signatures of lordship that they might well be thought of as integral components within a distinctive seigneurial 'package' of change. Secondly, it is clear that these ecological changes reflect far more than modes of exploitation that were favoured because they were somehow more efficient or productive. Rather, these changes can be argued to signal a fundamentally different sort of relationship between elite society and nature, with the desire to change and shape the flora and fauna of the countryside becoming part of the European aristocratic mindset.

Such a broader understanding of the ecological imprint of the European castle is something that we are only beginning to address, however. Bone assemblages from excavated sites have traditionally told us about the consumption of economic resources from hinterlands, as in archaeozoological terms seigneurial sites were 'top predators' in the medieval landscape

(Ervynck 1992). It is only now, however, that new research directions are paying attention to the social and symbolic importance of the living 'animalscape' as an extension of the material culture of aristocracy (Pluskowski 2007: 43-4). While this might initially seem a tangential concern it is clear that it was an essential aspect of a common aristocratic vocabulary that spanned diverse geographies. What we might hope to engage with more effectively in the future are the deeper levels of meaning that the physical display of such species and the practices of managing and hunting them afforded castle landscapes.

Viewing early castles: looking at, looking out

The development of social and symbolic approaches to medieval 'military' architecture has created an environment in which similarly nuanced interpretations of castle settings and how these too were perceived can hopefully flourish. While spatial analyses of castles have been refined methodologically and enriched theoretically since their first application in the 1960s, the implications of this mode of study for understanding relationships between noble buildings and their settings is only now being realised. There is good reason to think that domestic planning was not manipulated solely for the internal experience of built space, but sometimes with respect to surrounding landscapes.

That Romanesque great towers were intended to be highly visible is apparent not only from their physical locations but also their architecture. To take as one example: a recurring feature of eleventh- to early thirteenth-century donjons is the positioning of roofs well below the tops of parapets. This can only suggest that the powerful visual image of these towers – their wall-tops forming the skyline – featured prominently in the minds of builders. Examples have been identified from France, England, Ireland and Wales, but the phenomenon extends as far as Germany and Switzerland, as exemplified by the dramatically situated twelfth-century example of Neu Thierstein, located on a prominent rocky outcrop in the canton

Fig. 30. Part of the south elevation of the Norman White Tower of London, showing Romanesque windows at the upper level which mark a 'false' upper storey.

of Solothurn (Manning 2002). The exemplar is, however, the White Tower of London (Fig. 30) – a high-rise embodiment in stone of Norman royal dominance over a low-rise city of timber, its lavish Romanesque elevations also looming large over the river-borne approach to the city. Recent discoveries of early roof-lines within the structure show that the original Norman design featured a 'false' upper storey lined with dummy windows that rose above the level of the enclosed roof, giving the illusion that the lived-in space was more imposing and elevated than it really was (Impey 2008: 84-5).

Surveillance was an important function of early castle towers and not entirely for defensive reasons; it was a statement of power in its own right and arguably shows aspirations towards social control. The notion of panoptic surveillance (that is, an 'all seeing' gaze whereby a small number of people can observe and control a much larger group) is usually thought of as a phenomenon of the modern age. The idea is exemplified by Foucault's famous re-interpretation of Jeremy Bentham's

6. Theatres of Lordship: Noble Lifestyles

'Panopticon' – a utopian device for monitoring prison populations (Foucault 1980: 155). The castle as an instrument for landscape surveillance for reasons of economic control is one line of approach that has been pursued to good effect. On the Oisans massif in Alpine France, for example, landscape archaeology has shown the importance of intervisibility between lordly sites, valley-bottom communication routes and settlements associated with mineral exploitation, as with the twelfth-century 'shell keep' of Brandes (Bailly-Maître 2004). In central Appenninic Italy, survey and excavation have indicated that early castles were deliberately placed to overlooked *tratturi* (drove-roads) and hence control and tax the movement of shepherds and their vast flocks of sheep in transhumant medieval economies (Christie 2008). This notion of the castle as a toll collection point is exemplified by the dense concentration of castles – among the greatest anywhere in Europe – in the Middle Rhine valley, many of which originated as *Zollburg* ('toll-castles') for control of the wine trade, while the positioning of castle baileys across routeways through the Swiss Alps occurs for similar reasons.

Important antecedents for the surveillance functions of castle towers might be found in Carolingian palaces. Relevant here is Notker Balbus' account, written in the 880s, of the enigmatic *solarium* at Aachen. Described as a room from which Charlemagne could observe the comings and goings of palace dignitaries, perhaps from a window but more likely a balcony or covered gallery, this was evidently an elevated space – socially as well as physically – with a commanding gaze (De Jong 2008). While its location is unknown, an intriguing possibility is that Charlemegne's sun-room was accommodated in the squat donjon-like block that interrupted the *porticus* between the *aula regis* and the church (see p. 56). *Solaria* are documented at other Carolingian *villae*, perhaps indicating equivalent structures.

A related line of enquiry – still limited as yet – is showing how planning arrangements within European *donjons* provide evidence that rooftop panoramas were intended to be reached

Fig. 31. Donjon of Langeais, showing the position of a balcony-type structure at the upper level.

from private chambers and that access to them was hence a lordly prerogative (McNeill 2006). A close relationship clearly existed between domestic planning more generally and the 'design' of surrounding pleasure grounds. The idea of looking out on to the designed landscape from windows and vantage points within buildings is one that we have only recently begun to take seriously. Aesthetic sensibilities were not somehow absent from the minds of early castle builders. For example, at Langeais (Indre-et-Loire) the donjon of AD 1000 featured an external timber gallery linked to the living space on the upper storey (Fig. 31); built across the east face of the building between two projecting towers, it has been interpreted as a belvedere-type feature, from which exquisite views over the Loire valley could be admired (Impey and Lorans 1998: 68, 94). To external observers this side of the donjon presented a strikingly ordered and symmetrical architectural composition, rising above its naturally dominant setting.

The donjon at Loches (pp. 59-61) also had a gallery on the upper part of its south front, its level indicated by a line of joist holes, while the flanking galleries either side of the tenth-century hall and tower at Mayenne (pp. 73-6) also bear comparison. A similar projection of authority – active, outward and public – is evidenced in a British context by balcony-type features in the upper levels of Norman great towers at Chepstow (Monmouthshire), Corfe (Dorset) and Norwich (Norfolk), suggesting staged appearances to assembled audiences, although the late eleventh-century hall block at Richmond (North Yorkshire) featured galleries on two sides that overlooked the more private prospect of gardens and the river valley (Goodall 2011: 90).

The construction of such buildings in the medieval imagination has generally been sidelined in castle studies in favour of understanding how they were constructed 'in reality'. Yet the two are inescapably entwined, and the image of the castle embodied in romance literature provides an important context for understanding the multiple meanings of these views. For example, the hugely popular poems of Chrétien de Troyes in the late twelfth century are full of strikingly romanticised images of castles looming above parks, forests, lakes and rivers; in *Perceval,* the episode 'The Wondrous Bed' sees Gawain marvelling at the beauty of wooded hunting landscapes through windows on several occasions (Cline 1985: 201, 213). Crucially, a two-way process was at work: medieval literary sources inevitably drew on real-life examples, but landscapes too might have been manipulated with literary models in mind, although research has barely begun to take this into account. Fuller exploitation of medieval literary evidence is crucial for addressing contemporary perceptions and experiences of these spaces and for a more balanced understanding of castles as cultural artefacts of the Middle Ages.

A further challenge for the future is to question whether castles of earth and timber and those in the possession of more petty lords were located with an eye on their visual connections with territories. But we should also be cautious: the often open nature of castle earthworks in today's landscapes disguises the fact that during their functioning lifetimes these sites provided quite limited opportunities for experiencing the world beyond them; in a compact crowded site such as Hen Domen (Montgomeryshire), the countryside would have been visible only from the bailey walkway and the motte-top, and it was clearly the latter view which was most privileged (Higham and Barker 2000: 178).

Summary

The importance of portable material culture as a resource for understanding elite identities is under-valued in castle studies, while assemblages of animal bones can tell use about the distinctive ecological signature of lordship as well as the role diet played in emerging aristocratic culture. Building-focused approaches to castles do not necessarily have to be inward looking, and analyses of architectural space also have much to tell us about elite attitudes to the countryside these sites overlooked. A new avenue for research concerns the visual qualities of these sites, which clearly worked in both directions: castles were icons that were meant to be seen, but undervalued is the fact that they also allowed their elite patrons privileged access to elevated views, whether staged appearances to assembled throngs, or more distant views over scenery.

7

The Broader Context: Landscape and Townscape

Early castles were integral not only to a reordering of medieval society, but also the restructuring of the countryside. This legacy is everywhere. Castile and Catalonia took their names from the word 'castle', as did countless settlements that grew up at the feet of castles, reflected in common place-names such as 'Castelnau' in France, 'Neuburg' in Germany and 'Castelnuovo' in Italy. Coincident with the studding of Europe's rural landscape with private castles was the emergence of a new administrative geography characterised by 'castellanies' (districts centred on castles). Settlement historians have long appreciated the contribution of castles to the making of the European medieval countryside, and increasingly the horizons of castellology are extending to consider the places of these sites within their rural environments. A more radical view still is that we might consider rejecting castle study as a discrete field of scholarship entirely and instead consider them as lordship sites forming part and parcel of the total pattern of urban and rural settlement.

This chapter examines the place of castles in the European countryside and the agency of lordship in its transformation between the ninth and eleventh centuries. While there certainly did not exist any sort of monolithic template for an idealised European castle landscape that lords strived to make real, a keynote of this chapter is that we can detect a number of common underlying themes that together characterise the spatial ordering of these buildings and their settings. It considers the dynamic between castle and landscape at different scales, including the territories within which castles were set and the settlements in whose transformation their lords were often intimately involved.

Putting early castles in their places

To most archaeologists studying the medieval countryside it is the notion of regional difference that characterises the rural scene – the landscape of farms, hamlets, fields and villages that varied in kaleidoscopic fashion between different zones. The roles of castles in the workings and making of these landscapes were myriad. But in essence this has been understood from one of two perspectives. Whatever the military functions of early castles, most research now acknowledges that these sites were also working centres of manorial administration and agricultural management; in certain contexts their construction was also synonymous with colonising movements and the planning or re-planning of villages and other settlements. Often seen as complementary is the role of early castles in schemes of land improvement, woodland clearance and agricultural intensification. This notion of castles as active elements within the settlement pattern, rooted within the everyday working world, might seem at odds with their other prominent role, in what might be termed the 'aristocratic landscape'. This is the second way of thinking about the subject: castles as the focal points within a wider aristocratic *domaine*; centres of high-quality living where the nobility secluded and segregated themselves from communities in surroundings that showcased the trappings of aristocratic power, including parks, ponds and gardens. Neither of these views alone is adequate, and truly holistic studies of castles must take account of the multifarious ways these sites interfaced with their social and material environments, invariably presenting different faces of lordship to different audiences.

Our understanding of the place of the castle in the making of the medieval countryside has advanced unevenly, however. Across Europe as a whole, a key area of contrast regards the

126

7. The Broader Context: Landscape and Townscape

priorities of medieval archaeologists working on early medieval high-status sites and rural settlements either side of the former Iron Curtain. In former Communist states, ideological imperatives to engage with archaeologies of the 'common people' meant that a relative wealth of information is available on service settlements attached to Slavic elite fortresses of the early Middle Ages in countries including Poland and the Czech Republic (Ettel 2008: 166; Curta 2009: 39). A key site in this regard is the stronghold and settlement of Tornow (Kreis Calau) (Fig. 32) excavated in the former German Democratic Republic by J. Herrmann. Social stratification is reflected in the seventh- to ninth-century phases by the separation of a small circular stronghold of a Slavic noble from an open settlement beyond its defences, featuring workshops for industry and craftworking as well as housing an agricultural community. The centrepiece of the castle-like complex was a large central dwelling within a courtyard around which granaries, storerooms and accommodation for a small retinue were arrayed in radial fashion (Herrmann 1966; Brachmann 1983: 93-4). This stands in stark comparison to the situation in parts of Western Europe where for many years it was mainly the elite rural sites of the Carolingian world – palaces and estate centres – that constituted our greatest area of knowledge, with attendant settlements attracting less attention until much more recently.

In certain contexts castle study is virtually inseparable from rural settlement history. Although serious study of later medieval landscape is still relatively young in Ireland, medieval archaeologists here have long seen castles as an integral part of the rural economy. They perpetuated a long-established dispersed settlement pattern, today constitute its principal surviving vestiges, and remain critical resources for its study (O'Conor 1998: 1-17). Another case in point is the contribution of Tuscan archaeologists, led by the late Riccardo Francovich and the Area di Archeologia Medievale at Siena University, in revealing the place of castles in the total settlement pattern of central Italy as it shifted through the medieval centuries.

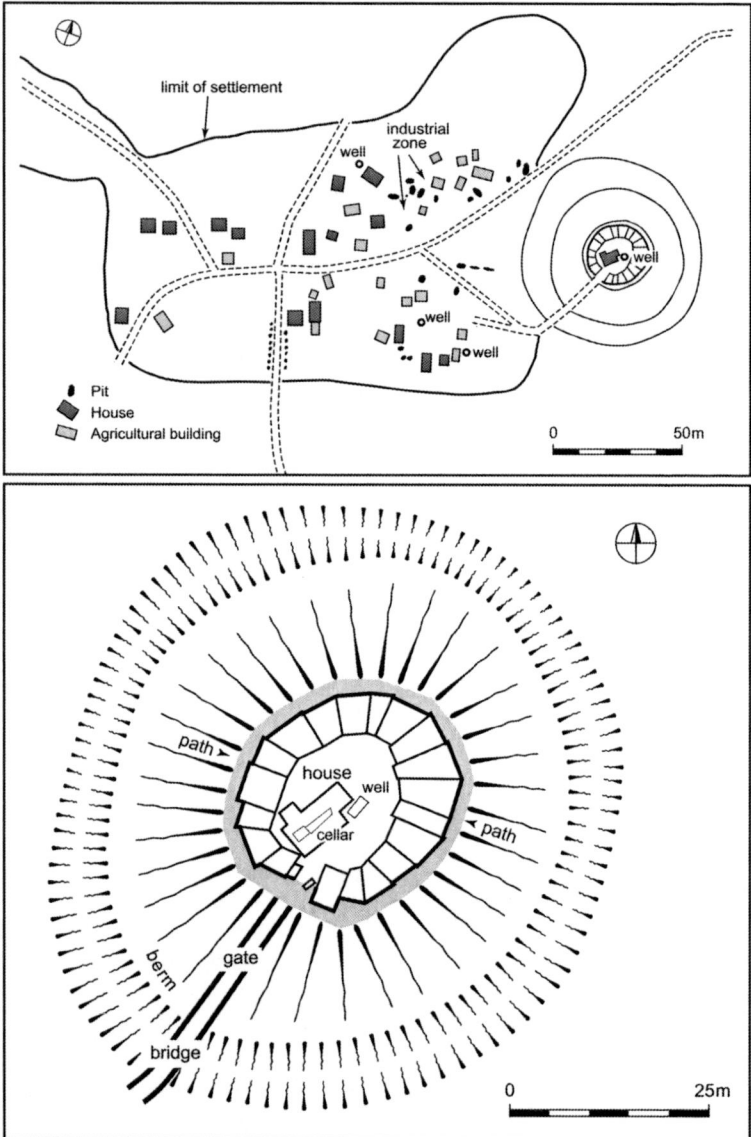

Fig. 32. Tornow, Germany: a Slavic ringwork with an attached settlement, as revealed by excavation.

128

7. The Broader Context: Landscape and Townscape

Large-scale regional survey allied to excavation has produced new data of sufficient quality and quantity to enable archaeologists to challenge old paradigms about *incastellamento* (the nucleation of hilltop villages, often next to private castles or *castelli* – although the word could also denote a fortified settlement: see pp. 140-5) and to develop new models for rural settlement evolution (Francovich 2008). Part of the reason for this is of course the sheer ubiquity of castles in the region – there were over 1,500 *castelli* in Tuscany by the fourteenth century, characteristically perched on highly visible hilltops.

Capita, *church and court*

As well as representing the interests of a powerful individual at a given point in time, over many generations a castle marked and memorialised entire noble dynasties. Particularly important in this context are some fundamental changes that were occurring within the structure of elite families in the immediate post-Carolingian period as recognised by the French historian Georges Duby (1977: 56-66). What he styled as the 'triumph of lineage' saw primogenital succession – the custom of the first-born inheriting an estate – becoming the norm over large parts of Western Europe by the twelfth century. As well as underpinning the rise of a much more settled aristocracy, this process also saw castles become inheritable assets. The cognate result was a strengthening link between family and locality that came to be embodied by the castle.

A common reflection of this was the adoption by the new nobility of toponymic surnames (i.e. referring to particular places or geographical features). Quite naturally, the names of numerous dynasties referenced the *capita* of their lordships as represented by castles, affording these sites another layer of meaning as monuments that celebrated ancestral links to the land, real or imagined, and proclaimed these to wider populations. As we have seen (p. 76), castles of the tenth and eleventh centuries were not necessarily intended to look 'new'; indeed, it is quite the reverse in some cases, and it is not out of the question that in some instances a false sense of antiquity was fostered to bolster the claims of families to their lands. This pattern was not uniform across Europe, however. In the sorts of kin-based Gaelic societies that characterised large parts of Ireland and Scotland during this period, customs of partible inheritance counted against the construction of permanent lordship sites in stone right up until the tower house phenomenon of the fifteenth century, with lordship expressed in fundamentally different ways.

Across most of Europe, distinctive landscape elements found in association with fortified *capita* accentuated and celebrated the link between family and territory. The European countryside is dotted with early private castles standing by churches that originated as *Eigenkirchen* ('private churches') and served as noble mausolea. Excavation has revealed representative examples of churches within eleventh-century castral complexes at Gemert in the Netherlands, for example, where the structure was of timber and occupied a moated island, and the Château de Chimay in Belgium, where it was stone-built and served as the necropolis for the Chimay family. The characteristic 'twinning' of castle and monastery also started early. Far more than a statement of the benefactor's piety, a new monastery founded within sight of the lordship centre became another enduring symbol of the noble family whose traditional place of burial it invariably became. An instructive early example is the foundation by Fulk Nerra, Count of Anjou, of a monastery named *Belli Locus* ('place of battle') a little over a kilometre from the fortified centre of Loches. The tall and elaborate church – built 1005-7, consecrated 1012, and topped with a great lantern tower – acted as a visual counterpart to the great donjon whose construction started only a few years later (see p. 31). It served as place of burial for one of Europe's greatest and early castle-builders; Fulk was interred within a tomb with *gisant* (a recumbent effigy) in a suitably antique style (Bachrach 1993: 101).

The key period of early castle growth was also broadly coincident with the emergence of seigneurial courts as the principal venues for the administration of rural justice. The first half of the eleventh century in particular saw the *placitum* (public court or assembly – also known as the *mallus* in the Frankish world) either disappear or arrogated to become the tribunal of the private lord, as well attested across areas of Western Europe extending from the Low Countries across France to northern Italy and Catalonia. Historians have hotly debated whether the usurpation of judicial institutions was sudden and radical or more protracted in nature. What is certain, however, is that it saw castellans profiting by exacting fines, while as an institution the castle became an emblem of justice in its own right because its hall was the venue for courts.

Castles and the making of settlement landscapes

That this chapter focuses on the rural scene is quite deliberate, as early castle-building was essentially a rural phenomenon. The towers built by noblemen and patrician families which studded the skylines of townscapes, particularly in southern Europe, were predominantly a later phenomenon, rare before the twelfth and thirteenth centuries. In the early medieval period, bishops, kings and other rulers built and maintained urban strongholds in major centres that sometimes equated to hybrid castle-palaces, as at Ghent and Tours, while private lords on occasion maintained residences (sometimes defended, to greater and lesser extents) within major towns that were themselves walled. Exceptional was the case of Louis IV's siege in 938 of a comtal *arx* or stronghold built within the city of Laon in Picardy, which he replaced with his own citadel (Purton 2009: 146).

These developments should not deflect us from the fact that Europe's new aristocracy was predominantly rural-based, with interests tied to new rather than old settlements. In southern Europe, for example, there is good reason to think that the emergence of private power and the first castles was especially rapid in precisely those regions with few cities. In Italy, Christopher Wickham has suggested that in the north of the country urban public authority effectively held back the establishment of private lordships in the ninth and tenth centuries, while the process was accelerated in the south through the absence of cities that acted as effective units of political power, so that developments here more closely resemble the situation in France and the Low Countries (1981: 162-3). On the whole, early private fortifications are notable for their segregation from populations and for their avoidance of established urban centres, although in numerous cases new castles became hubs for markets and their baileys points for commercial growth.

It is as part and parcel of a more general phenomenon of the increasing visibility of lordship sites that the builders of early private fortifications made their mark on society and landscape, their physical elevation and defences becoming hallmarks of social separateness and distinction. In certain types of landscapes the topographical elevation of lordly sites above communities could itself carry social messages. In Austria, for example, the term *Vertikalverschiebung* (vertical shift/displacement) has been used to describe the re-location of castles to more elevated locations from *c.* 1100, for security but also the tangible display of social distance between the nobility and subordinate social groups, while the entire *incastellamento* phenomenon in southern Europe can be considered in a similar light (pp. 140-5).

Archaeological investigations have often shown the notion of the castle imposed upon a settlement to be misleading as their construction so often marked one phase – in some cases the culmination – of a much longer-term sequence of high-status occupation. Over the *longue durée* castles were part of a much longer-term trend towards the increasing visibility and clearer definition of elite sites within their communities that was stirring long before. In this sense, the castle is but one manifestation of much broader phenomenon with antecedents in the *Herrenhöfen* (large chiefly farmsteads, often enclosed) of the fourth and fifth centuries, continued through developments in Carolingian settlements of the seventh and eighth centuries and beyond, which saw high-status residences become increasingly differentiated within rural settlements whose plans were themselves progressively more ordered. In archaeological terms, the 'arrival' of Europe's earliest castles within rural settlements represented an evolution not a revolution of spatial order and we should be careful not to single out their construction as the root cause of change; it was one link in a much more complex chain of causation.

This was manifested most commonly through the demarcation and zoning of lordship sites within settlements and through their characteristic physical association with churches and chapels, which became such a characteristic feature of the rural scene. The notion of a church physically annexed to the early castle is part of a wider phenomenon whereby proprietary foundations were located close to noble residences, although in these cases the association between lordship and religious piety was even more apparent, with the church tower a visual complement to the castle tower and the church invariably located at the junction between the seigneurial zone and the public space of the settlement. Despite the enormous variety of castle designs, shapes and sizes, an essential characteristic many have in common is the rounded, enclosed forms which marked them out as distinctive from rural settlements (Svensson 2008: 327-43).

More generally, it is increasingly widely recognised that castles were not only elements of the settlement pattern, but – through the agency of their owners – catalysts for change in the countryside. In their key synthesis of the rural landscape of medieval Western Europe, Chapelot and Fossier saw the castle as the most important factor of all in the nucleation of rural communities (1985: 129). Morphogenetic studies of 'existing' villages show how varied could be the structure of the castral village. In south-west France, for example, the creation of eleventh- and twelfth-century settlements sometimes involved the imposition of circular forms on the landscape, divided in radial fashion into plots, as at the *Castrum* de Mirebeau (Allier) (Fig. 33), where three concentric circular enclosures around a central motte, the outermost *c.* 700m across, formed a morphological frame for the village (Querrien 2008: 129-31).

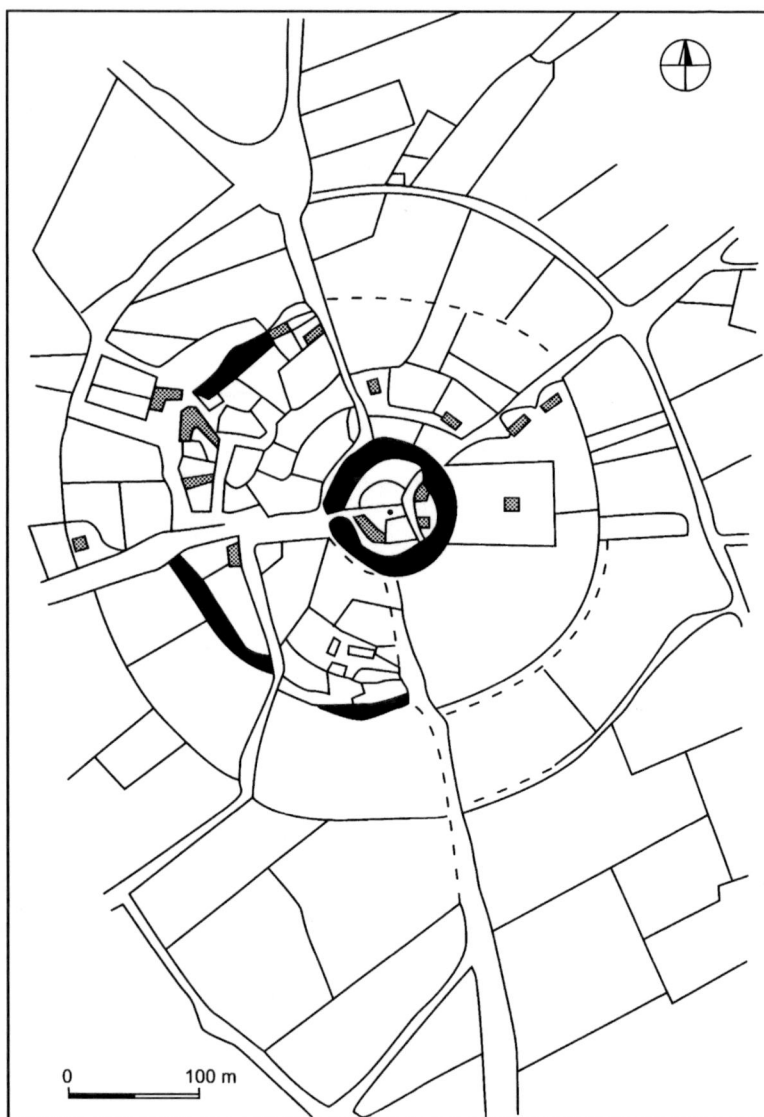

Fig. 33. Radial planned village and field system around a motte at Mirebeau in southern France.

7. The Broader Context: Landscape and Townscape

A useful concept here is that of *encellulement* (or 'cell-formation') favoured by French historians (Fossier 1982: 288-595), but writ large over north-west Europe. It denotes the emergence of tightly-focused structures of power based on organised *terroirs* (or lands) and fixed castles, villages and parishes within an otherwise decentralised world. Perhaps our foremost archaeological case study that embodies this narrative of the turn of the first millennium AD as a critical horizon in rural settlement history is the site of Colletière, lying on the southern edge of Lake Paladru near Charavines (Isère) and excavated by Michel Colardelle. This long-term archaeological rescue and research project is remarkable not only for the exceptional preservation of material remains from an underwater context, but for the exceptionally close integration of different lines of archaeological enquiry to reveal the intricacies of the site's social and economic life and its context within a dynamic settlement history (Colardelle and Verdel 1993). A fortified timber complex on the lake edge (Fig. 34) had a remarkably short lifespan, established in the first years of the eleventh century but abandoned by *c.* 1040 as it was superseded by a new settlement pattern and related administrative system of castellanies focused on hilltop mottes.

Two points that have emerged from this remarkable project are pertinent here. First, while the site of Colletière is precastral, it was both defended and seigneurial in character. Comprising a rectangular palisaded enclosure of 1300m², the compound showed clear evidence of social differentiation; a principal hall for the leading family is juxtaposed with structures used by a socially subservient population, with artisanal facilities and a rich assemblage of agricultural tools confirming a bustling working centre. Second, the network of mottes that replaced these lakeside settlements was active for a very limited period – as indicated by the excavated example less than a kilometre away at Châtelard – to be replaced by the end of the eleventh century with a smaller number of stone castles, which in many cases became nucleation points for more permanent settlements. The only equivalent seigneurial site to Colletière

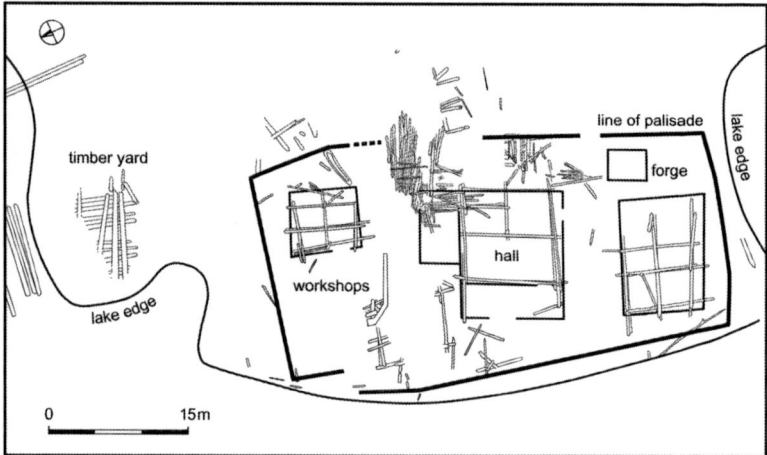

Fig. 34. Colletière, Charavines: a fortified seigneurial complex of the early eleventh century on the shores of Lake Paladru.

in terms of conditions of preservation is the late tenth- to twelfth-century motte and bailey of Pineuilh (Gironde), where excavations by INRAP (the French National Institute for Preventive Archaeological Research) in advance of road building in 2002-3 uncovered startlingly well-preserved waterlogged timberwork including a footbridge, providing invaluable information about carpentry technologies and woodland management practices.

The nearest German equivalent to *encellulement* is *die Verdorfung*: the origin of villages through the concentration of previously more scattered rural populations. Again, it is the increasingly bounded nature of social space, the orderliness of settlement plans and the focal role of elite sites that emerge as keynotes of the process. Also important in this context are what medieval archaeologists in central and eastern Europe have termed 'service settlements' of the ninth and tenth centuries – villages of craftspeople and peasants attached to royal or ducal fortresses, as exemplified by sites such as Pohansko near Bøeclav (Czech Republic) and Pliska (Bulgaria) (Curta 2009). As nucleations of population apparently forced by elite agency, debate has focused on whether these service settlements represent a distinctively eastern European phenomenon as opposed to a distinctive form of a practice that was ultimately Carolingian in origin. What is important here is their broader pan-European context: although the populations of these sites were seemingly not physically enclosed or annexed to elite sites with fortifications, they are part and parcel of the same broad 'encellment' of population.

A particularly important theme here is the critical status of baileys as points of interface between castle and territory, although this has only recently received detailed attention in some areas. The seigneurial 'resources' contained within baileys might have underestimated significance as features of social control and display, although we are only starting to characterise them as such. Detailed study of baileys in Belgium shows that these were often vast spaces completely unsuited to defence; the movement of residences into lower baileys from the eleventh and twelfth centuries often saw the expansion and further compartmentalisation of bailey space, which took in features of lordship such as mills and frequently acted as urban nucleation points (Mignot et al. 2004). Deserted or shifted medieval settlements within castle baileys have particularly great potential for study; excavation and fieldwork is frequently showing that in the eleventh and twelfth centuries in particular these were not necessarily urban or rural in the strict sense, but sometimes of seigneurial character, tied to the workings of the castle.

A related consideration is that while the environs of castles might readily be characterised as 'landscapes of power', easily overlooked is the evidence these might provide for limitations to lordly authority and even resistance to it. For example, how often might the evidence of deserted settlements appended to private castles or lying within baileys tell us that 'forced' nucleations under the shadow of fortresses were unsustainable ventures in the face the agency of peasants? A thought provoking case study of precisely this, based on archaeological investigation and documentary research, is the landscape of the 'co-seigneury' of Mouret (Aveyron, France), where lordly policy failed to achieve castle-focused nuclei at four sites in the area and the settlement pattern remained predominantly dispersed (Ferrand 2006). Many of the elements of the 'aristocratic landscape' – mills and parks, for example – can also be conceptualised as arenas for contestation between lords and communities. There are other potential ways that archaeological researchers might engage with notions of peasant individuality and agency behind the unity and regulation that image of the seigneurial village outwardly presents. Although the topic is under-researched, potential indicators of low-level resistant identities include the illegal possession of hand-mills, investment in individualistic dress accessories and the presence on peasant holdings of stones robbed from lordly sites (Smith 2009). In other contexts, we might seek evidence of poaching in animal bone assemblages from rural sites, or for continuity in traditional practices under the shadows of colonial castles.

We should also not neglect the fact that castles also played active roles in the evolutions of non-nucleated landscapes. In twelfth- and thirteenth-century Moray, in northern Scotland, for example, mottes and enterprising Flemish colonists 'went hand in hand' to open up this landscape to more intensive pastoral exploitation (Oram 2006: 296). More often, colonising early castles are found in the context of wetland and, in particular, woodland reclamation, although we should be careful not to caricature their role in the semi-mythical 'quest for land' running up to *c.* 1300. In Germany especially there is an enduring tradition of seeing early castles built in wilderness locations – forests, marshes and bare hilltops – as symbolising the pioneering spirit of aristocratic families. In the Rhine-Main region, for example, seigneurial castles of the eleventh century sprang up on the edges of the *Altsiedelland* ('old settlement land') at the interface of the new areas being claimed and cleared by ministerial families (Friedrich 2006: 150).

In Switzerland so-called 'land-clearance castles' (*Rodungsburgen*) are among the earliest noble fortifications so far identified, dating to the mid-tenth and early eleventh centuries and including examples such as Altenberg at Füllinsdorf, which was already abandoned by *c.* 1100 (Meyer 1994: 305). In the densely forested Spessart area of Germany, regional survey is revealing the active role of castles in settlement expansion and in organising activities such as hunting and iron production; the region contains perhaps up to 250 sites, mostly modest castles of the gentry classes, with a key period of construction in the twelfth and thirteenth centuries (Kemethmüller 2011). Archaeologists have looked for corroborating evidence in their excavations; the site of Salbüel, in the canton of Luzern (Switzerland) showed a timber castle (here an oval-shaped palisaded enclosure of the eleventh and twelfth centuries) to have been built over a charcoal layer interpreted as evidence of slash-and-burn style clearance (Zeune 1996: 148-9).

These considerations aside, we should be careful not to think of a European 'norm' for the early castle landscape. In some regions the 'seascape' was as important as the landscape in the expression of lordly power, while in other regions inland lakes were favoured and had enduring associations with authority. In Finland, Norway and Sweden, for example, castles were predominantly built on coastal and island sites rather than on hilltops in the supposedly 'classic' European style. To engage with constructions of power and elite identity within these settings we must put the sea 'centre stage' (Van de Noort 2011: 3). Burgeoning research on the Gaelic landscapes and settlements of Ireland is revealing distinctive relationships between lordship and landscape where classic Western European-style fortresses were lacking and where dynasts expressed their power in fundamentally different ways to the mainstream. In a culture of lordship where genealogy and poetry were more important for bolstering elite power than permanent masonry castles, the settings of Gaelic power centres not uncommonly referenced the heritage of earlier ritual landscapes and early Christian inauguration sites. In Scotland also, it is only quite recently that fresh research directions are paying attention to the complex psychological dimensions of lordly landscapes where Gaelic traditions were strong and Anglo-French models are unhelpful for understanding the notion of a 'castle landscape' (Oram 2008: 355-6).

Debating incastellamento

The centrality of castles to the making of medieval Mediterranean landscapes is particularly well attested. The classic *incastellamento* model developed by Toubert (1973) on the basis of research in central Italy saw new hilltop settlements forming around small towers or *roccas* on elevated positions between the ninth and eleventh centuries; they were understood as the products of lordly initiative, signalling a major re-location of formerly more dispersed rural populations to fortified villages. Physically, these settlements usually comprised crammed arrangements of narrow houses and streets, often equipped with purpose-built cisterns and sometimes industrial zones, clinging to rocky eminences beneath castles and (very often) their associated churches. The *incastellemanto* phenomenon was manifested in numerous regionally and micro-regionally distinctive forms, the most obvious area of variation being the degree of intimacy between castle and village. In some instances houses clustered in concentric fashion around a central castral nuclei; in others, they grew up at the foot of the castle on a lower point or stretched away in linear fashion; elsewhere, settlements were less concentrated, with the seigneurial centre more loosely associated with multiple *villae*. At a wider scale, this process was tied to the breakup of the ancient landscape and the emergence of a new structure (the *curtis*) for organising the countryside.

Incastellamento entailed a surge of castle building; new fortifications 'multiplied in waves moving from south to north' (Bisson 2009: 41). The early heartlands in the tenth century were Italy and Provence, with important and parallel developments affecting Spain during approximately the same period and slightly later equivalents in southern France and ultimately around the Loire and the Rhine. To take as one example the mountainous southern French Vivrais region: here some 80% of private castles were associated with a *habitat subordonné* (dependent settlement), although the pattern of *incastellamento* was both drawn out and intricately varied between localities, with a wide array of forms taken by castle villages and hamlets, both enclosed and non-enclosed (Laffont 2009).

Excavation and field survey have furnished us with numerous case studies of seigneurially led village formation between the eleventh and fourteenth centuries that are widely dispersed across north-west Europe (Hansson 2006: 135-60). One of our foremost exemplars is the Tuscan *incastellamento* village of Rocca San Silvestro, where the seigneurial presence was associated with mineral extraction and metalworking. The 'perched villages' of Provence furnish us with other dramatic examples of settlements that apparently originated as seigneurially-forced nucleations. The deserted settlement of Rougiers, in Provence, south-east France, investigated over several seasons of detailed research excavation in the 1960s might be seen as the embodiment of the hilltop village (Fig. 35). Formed in the late twelfth century beneath a dramatically situated castle, the settlement displays a regulated form, with house plots bereft of yards or gardens planned on a lower level to the seigneurial site, which embraced the chapel within its basse-cour (bailey) and overlooked the community's water supply in the form of a cistern (Démians d'Archimbaud 1981).

In Spain, a further characteristic aspect to the re-ordering of rural settlements around fortified nuclei was the provision of sophisticated irrigation systems, sometimes involving artificial canals and integrating milling facilities with the supply of water for agriculture. This is well attested in Catalonia as well as Al-Andalus between the ninth and eleventh centuries, with both Muslim *husûn* and Christian *castra* commonly controlling irrigated zones as well as settlements that occupied (or re-occupied) prominent physical positions. This is one very good reason why we should not conceptualise *incastellamento*-style

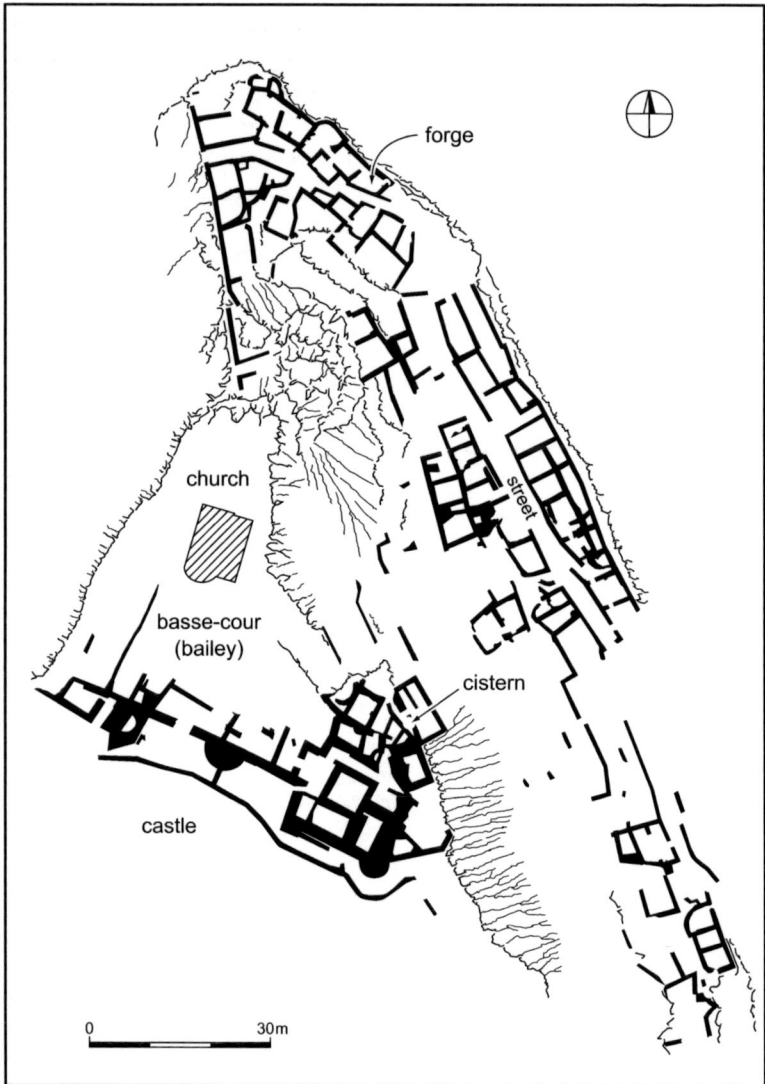

Fig. 35. Plan of the hilltop village of Rougiers, as revealed by archaeological survey and excavation.

Fig. 36. Remains of a medieval house within the 'perched' hilltop village of Rougiers.

settlements as 'feudal' villages: in early medieval Spain parallel developments were occurring in areas under Islamic control that were characterised by kin-based (and explicitly non-feudal) societies; indeed, since the 1980s the bulk of archaeological case studies have come from these regions (Glick 1995: 109-10).

We should take care not to caricature the image of the ordered seigneurial village, however. Easily overlooked is evidence of idiosyncrasy and individualism in plot histories, with buildings showing their own distinctive biographies of building and rebuilding. An encastellated peasant was not necessarily an oppressed peasant, submissive and powerless beneath the shadow of the castle (Fig. 36). We should not overlook the benefits that the new structure bought with it: customary fixed rents (often modest), and a more communal and secure way of living that may even have positively fostered solidarity in the face of authority.

The essential *incastellamento* model continues to be refined as new information emerges to flesh out and in some cases challenge our understanding of a phenomenon initially studied

143

largely through documents (especially charters). It is now quite clear that different regions display variations on the underlying pattern. Even in Lazio, the region studied by Toubert, the chronology of *incastellamento* was clearly varied; in the *Ager Veientanus* (the region around the former Roman city of Veii), for instance, villages were nucleating appreciably earlier. Perhaps the best studied region, however, is southern Tuscany, where a refined *incastellamento* model is emerging on the basis of excavations at the 'type-site' of Montarrenti, but also Miranduolo, Poggibonsi and Scarlino. This is seeing the emergence of many private fortifications from *within* villages in the tenth century and their transformation by the twelfth century into power centres affirming the status of the new aristocracy (Francovich and Hodges 2003). We also see social stratification emerging in other ways – through the differential building of structures in stone; through the construction of long-houses in settlement patterns dominated by huts; and through the planning of fortified granaries. The key refinement of earlier models is that many *incastellamento*-style villages were re-cast from earlier permanent settlements, often timber-built and comprising nucleations of dwellings, workshops and storage areas, that pre-dated the castle presence; out of 41 fortified sites or *castelli* in Tuscany investigated archaeologically, two-thirds (27) reveal significant early medieval phases, and in some cases rural settlements were already migrating towards hilltop positions in the seventh and eighth centuries (Francovich 2008: 67-9).

Another reason for caution is that in Italy at least, documented *castelli* were not necessarily seigneurial castles, and similar arguments could be applied to other parts of southern Europe. The term means 'fortified village', and some such settlements were orientated around defended monasteries, as in the case of the thoroughly excavated site of San Vincenzo al Volturno, for example, or even churches. Revisionist approaches to the *incastellamento* phenomenon point out that *accentramento* (the centralisation of populations) could occur without the presence of fortifications and could involve the cooperative actions of peasants rather than being seigneuri-ally-led (Wickham 1985). As in other contexts across Europe, we should be aware of the limitations of monocausal explana-tions that single out lordship – and the presence of castles – as the sole stimulus for settlement change. In some cases we can question whether the driving force behind *incastellamento* was the re-organisation of peasant ag-riculture rather than a cranking up of social control, as local lords sought to maximise profits from estates and drive to-wards greater efficiencies in agriculture. The pattern of *incastellamento* in Tuscany has led Francovich (2008: 63) to suggest that hilltop sites provided certain advantages for sus-tainable agriculture, including the resistance to erosion of rocky terraces and limiting the risk of poor harvests by farming multiple slopes. What is certain is that it is simplistic to as-sume that a military or defensive rationale explains the widespread occupation of hilltop sites in the period – that these locations were somehow inconvenient but safe. Rather, they were emblematic of a new attitude to territorial control linked to a characteristic system of landscape management. Over a longer timescale *incastellamento* may have accelerated a more protracted process whereby the balance between settlement in lowland and upland locations was shifting in emphasis towards the latter. It was not so much a 'village moment' as one stage in a longer-term transformation of the total settlement pattern, and castles were not so much catalysts for settlement change as elements in the re-orientation of the fabric of rural life. The presence of a village was not itself new; what was different was the development of its internal hierarchy as the *signoria* occu-pied favoured zones to enhance their prestige and raise their profile.

Summary

As distinctive features of complex design both physically and metaphysically elevated above working agricultural land-scapes, early castles symbolised division between lords and communities but were also integrated within the machinery of the rural economy. At a broader scale, early castle building was inextricably linked to the *encellulement* (encellment) of a European landscape whose organisation came to be characterised by essentially local structures of power. An underlying and unifying ideology of lordship ensured some important commonalities in how these structures interfaced with their settings. The most prominent manifestation of this was the spatial ordering of associated settlements, although we should be aware of the problems of singling out seigneurial agency in the formation of villages. Encastellation was also coincident with the privatisation of the workings of justice, which saw castles used as the venues for courts, while over the longer term they served as ancestral markers, being associated with parish churches and sometimes being visually and architecturally linked to monasteries.

8

Conclusions: The Rise of the Seigneury

When archaeologists and historians debated the origins of castles in the 1960s a key problem was that there were too few excavated sequences. The evidence base was limited to the extent that a single site could be contemplated as the mythical origin point for the castle-building phenomenon, as with Doué-la-Fontaine. The early picture presented by this and other classic case studies – which must also include Brian Hope-Taylor's investigations at Abinger in England and Adolf Herrnbrodt's at der Husterknupp in Germany – has now changed almost out of recognition. We need to respect the contributions of these seminal excavations but no longer defer to them, and the archaeology of early castles now amounts to much more than a quest for the earliest datable example of some type or other – although for the record the motte at Boves and the hall-tower complex at Mayenne, both reliably dated developments of *c.* 900, are particularly prodigious. Other findings, at places such as the *Castrum* d'Andone, Hen Domen, the Tour d'Albon and Sugny, to name but a few of the more influential projects, emphasise not only the enormous diversity of early castle-building practices but also the multi-layered social and economic lives of these places. Castle studies are now much more landscape aware and many such studies include sophisticated environmental analyses and considerations of settings that were far beyond the horizons of early excavators.

The huge growth in medieval archaeology means that we must confront some very different challenges to those that faced earlier scholars embroiled in the classic origins of the

castle debate: a large number of examples from different contexts, excavated and recorded in different ways according to
different research agendas, and published in different languages. Where does this leave us? A case study such as
Colletière, Charavines, points the way forward in many respects – a strikingly multi-faceted but remarkably integrated
programme of evolving long-term archaeological research that
does not necessarily have a single castle as its focus. Alongside
Riccardo Francovich's investigations at Rocca San Silvestro,
this project has emerged as an equivalent to the celebrated
Wharram Percy programme in northern England as an exemplar of total settlement history that allows the seigneurial
contribution to the making of medieval landscapes to be understood in context.

It is also within the context of their surrounding cultural
landscapes that the heritage value of many European castles is
being realised, as at Rocca San Silvestro, where the castle site
and fortified village are now the centrepiece of a park containing museums and trails that showcase the rich mineral
exploitation of the zone as revealed by landscape archaeology.
This concept has been emulated not only elsewhere in Italy but
also more widely in Europe. The presentation of individual
sites to the visiting public overwhelmingly concentrates on
military aspects of their heritage, however. The research findings of academics and other specialists working in the field
need to be reflected in the ways these monuments are presented to the public, in particular by various state agencies.

This book has stressed from the beginning that international research agendas are essential for the long-term health
of the subject – this is the most appropriate scale of enquiry for
understanding a progressively Europeanised aristocratic culture, while it is only through trans-national research that the
distinctiveness of individual regions comes into focus. We must
make sure that post-modernism does not dissolve away entirely the grand narrative tradition in archaeology. This book
has also put particular emphasis on the social context of early
castle-building, which is argued to be integral to the changing

8. Conclusions: The Rise of the Seigneury

self-perception of a more confident brand of social elite that was tied to specific territories. Castles certainly had multiple origins, both in time and space, although the notion of an elite ideology developing among the new aristocracy of medieval Europe provided a unifying force that ultimately bound these various developments together. While we are perfectly content to apply the art-historical label 'Romanesque' to tenth- and eleventh-century great towers in European castles and perhaps also to certain types of portable object that excavations within them might uncover, it would be odd – heretical even – to style timber castles or for that matter medieval villages and towns of the same period as 'Romanesque' (Roberts 2008: 269-73). But the conceptual leap is worth thinking about, given that all were products of a medieval culture with underlying unities, ranging from social and economic structures to aspects of religion and agricultural practice.

Another important focus of this book has been to examine the intersection between castles, whose underlying spatial ordering embodies at least a degree of pan-European homogeneity, and the working landscapes of the everyday – fields, farms and settlements – that display a kaleidoscopic variety of regional experiences. It has been argued that the study of European castles with this in mind – as components within their evolving cultural environments over the *longue durée* – can help us engage with the more complex issue of aristocratic attitudes to landscape and how these too changed through time. But in certain parts of Europe typological and morphological approaches hold sway; for many, the subject continues to lend itself to the production of castellological inventories, databases, maps and atlases that, no matter how nuanced or painstakingly assembled, cannot take us very far. Equally, while revisionist approaches are confronting militaristic frameworks of interpretation on several fronts, too easy is the temptation to reduce debates within castle studies to binary opposites, with 'social/symbolic' and 'military' at either end of a spectrum of interpretation that misrepresents medieval society's own views.

Recognition of castles as constituents within the total settlement pattern and of their baileys as points of interface with communities has nonetheless grown considerably, even if the further horizon, that of moving towards a more nuanced understanding of the psychology and symbolism of castle landscapes, seems more distant. In this sense, studies of castles within their wider settings arguably provide a platform for a much broader understanding of the aristocratic appropriation and manipulation of space in the middle ages, breaking down the artificial barriers that have traditionally compartmentalised castle study. In some senses the uniqueness of the castle is diminished: castles are one manifestation of the longer-term archaeology of power and its negotiation.

There are many promising areas for related research and future debate, including the status of castles as contested features of landscape (not necessarily in a martial sense), their place within the wider ecological imprint of lordship, and the lordly 'seascapes' that were a feature of life in many parts of Europe. We have dealt quite tangentially with the enhanced role scientific dating techniques can play in the castle origins debate, although mortar-dating (radiocarbon dating of lime mortars) is clearly an area with massive potential within castle studies, and we can only speculate as to how this could impact on our chronologies of masonry building. Virtual reality technologies and GIS-based analyses hold unrealised promise for coming to grips with medieval experiences of buildings and their settings *in toto*, while the potential of geophysical survey to explore the contexts of great towers and map the myriad activities within baileys is under-realised. Interplay with complementary fields of scholarship is also important, with fuller engagement with a wide body of medieval literary and art historical evidence particularly crucial if we are really serious about addressing contemporary perceptions and experiences of these spaces. Again, we might question the very status of castle studies as a discrete area of academic specialism, and for good reason.

Any sort of meaningful archaeological research agenda

needs to be more than a shopping list of sites. A major challenge for the future is to capitalise on the research potential of developer-led archaeological investigation that is now characteristic of many parts of Europe, rather than mourn the inexorable and widespread decline of long-term set-piece research excavations and those sponsored by heritage agencies to present sites to the public. It might seem paradoxical and deeply traditionalist that a volume focused on debate should end with a plea for further fieldwork and excavation, but alongside re-appraisals of our extant data set this too is critical for the health of the subject. Re-appraisals of sites such as Loches and the Tower of London show that there is still so much more to be teased out of even supposedly the best known structures, and it is sobering to note that while Hen Domen is probably Europe's most thoroughly investigated timber castle, only half the bailey was ever excavated. It reminds us that no matter how often we re-think the past, fresh information is ultimately medieval archaeology's lifeblood.

Bibliography

Aarts, B. (1996) 'Early castles of the Meuse-Rhine border region and some parallels in Western Europe *c.* 1000: a comparative approach', *Château Gaillard* 17: 11-23.

Aarts, B. (2007) 'Motte-and-bailey castles of Europe: some aspects concerning their origin and evolution', *Virtus: Jaarboek voor Adelsgeschiedenis* 14: 37-56.

Airlie, S. (1995) 'The aristocracy', in R. McKitterick (ed.), *The New Cambridge Medieval History*, vol. II: *c. 700-c. 900* (Cambridge: Cambridge University Press), 431-50.

Allen Brown, R. (1969) 'An historian's approach to the origins of the castle in England', *Archaeological Journal* 126: 131-48.

Allen Brown, R. (1976) *English Castles* (London: Batsford).

Anderson, W. (1970) *Castles of Europe: From Charlemagne to the Renaissance* (London: Elek).

Bachrach, B.S. (1993) *Fulk Nerra, the Neo-Roman Consul, 987-1040* (Berkeley and Los Angeles: University of California Press).

Bagge, S., Gelting, M.H. and Lindkvist, T. (eds) (2011) *Feudalism: New Landscapes of Debate* (Turnhout: Brepols).

Bailly-Maître, M-C. (2004) 'Fortifications ou structures de contrôle? Les reliefs aménagés du massif de l'Oisans', *Château Gaillard* 22: 13-26.

Barry, T. (2008) 'The study of medieval Irish castles: a bibliographic survey', *Proceedings of the Royal Irish Academy* 108: 115-36.

Barry, T., De Meulemeester, J. and Poisson, J-M. (2001) 'Recherches internationales sur le château de la Tour d'Albon (France)', in M. Valor and M.A. Carmona (eds), *European Symposium for Teachers of Medieval Archaeology 4* (Sevilla: Universidad de Sevilla), 129-36.

Bartlett, R. (1993) *The Making of Europe: Conquest, Colonization and Cultural Change 950-1350* (London: Penguin).

Basilio (2004) 'A pilgrimage to the Alcázar of Toledo: ritual, tourism and propaganda in Franco's Spain', in D. Madina Lasansky and B. McLaren (eds), *Architecture and Tourism: Perception, Performance and Place* (Oxford: Berg), 93-108.

Bibliography

Beresford, G. (1987) *Goltho: The Development of an Early Medieval Manor c. 850-1150* (London: HMSO).

Bisson, T.N. (2009) *The Crisis of the Twelfth Century. Power, Lordship and the Origins of European Government* (Princeton and Oxford: Princeton University Press).

Bloch, M. (1954) *The Historian's Craft* (Manchester: Manchester University Press).

Bloch, M. (1961) *Feudal Society*, vol. 2: *Social Classes and Political Organization*, tr. L.A. Manyon (London: Routledge and Kegan Paul).

Boucharlat, E. (2009) 'Panorama de l'archéologie castrale en France', *Revue Archéologique du Centre de la France* 48: 232-4.

Bourgeois, L. (ed.) (2009) *Une résidence des Comtes d'Angoulême autour de l'an mil: le* castrum *d'Andone (Villejoubert, Charente). Publications des Fouilles d'André Debourd (1971-1995)* (Caen: Publications du CRAHM).

Bouvier, A., Pinto, G., Pierre, G., Guibert, P., Nicolas-Méry, D. and Baylé, M. (2011) 'La datation par luminescence appliquée à l'architecture médiévale: la tour nord-est du donjon d'Avranches (Manche, France)', *ArchéoSciences* 34: 59-68.

Brachmann, H-J. (1983) 'Research into the early history of the Slav populations in the territory of the German Democratic Republic', *Medieval Archaeology* 27: 89-106.

Brather, S. (2004) 'The beginnings of Slavic settlement east of the river Elbe', *Antiquity* 78: 314-29.

Bur, M. (1982) 'The motte and bailey castle: instrument of a revolution', *Engineering and Science* 45.3: 11-14.

Caldwell, D.H., Hall, M.A. and Wilkinson, C.M. (2009) 'The Lewis hoard of gaming pieces: a re-examination of their context, meanings, discovery and manufacture', *Medieval Archaeology* 53: 155-203.

Campana, S., Dabas, M., Marasco, L., Piro, S. and Zamuner, D. (2009) 'Integration of remote sensing, geophysical surveys and archaeological excavation for the study of a medieval mound (Tuscany, Italy)', *Archaeological Prospection* 16: 167-76.

Christie, N. (2006) *From Constantine to Charlemagne: An Archaeology of Italy, AD 300-800* (Aldershot: Ashgate).

Christie, N. (2008) ' "Of sheep and men": castles and transhumance in the upper Sangro valley and in the Cicolano, Italy', in G. Lock and A. Faustoferri (eds), *Archaeology and Landscape in Central Italy. Papers in Memory of John A. Lloyd* (Oxford: OUSA Monographs), 105-20.

Chapelot, J. and Fossier, R. (1985) *The Village and House in the Middle Ages,* tr. H. Cleere (Berkeley/Los Angeles).

Bibliography

Cline, R.H. (1985) *Chrétien de Troyes: Perceval or the Story of the Grail* (Athens: University of Georgia Press).

Colardelle, M. and Verdel, E. (1993) *Les habitats du lac de Paladru (Isère) dans leur environnement: La formation d'un terroir au XIe siècle* (Paris: Editions de la Maison des Sciences de l'Homme).

Costambeys, M., Innes, M. and MacLean, S. (2011) *The Carolingian World* (Cambridge: Cambridge University Press).

Coulson, C. (1996) 'Cultural realities and reappraisals in English castle-study', *Journal of Medieval History* 2: 171-208.

Creighton, O.H. (2005) *Castles and Landscapes: Power, Community and Fortification in Medieval England* (London: Equinox).

Creighton, O.H. (2009) *Designs upon the Land: Elite Landscapes of the Middle Ages* (Woodbridge: Boydell).

Crespi, L., Enaud, F., Meyer, W. and Taylor, A. (1975) *Glossaire Burgenfachwörterbuch des mittelalterlichen Wehrbaus* (Frankfurt am Main: Verlag Wolfgang Weidlich).

Crouch, D. (2005) *The Birth of Nobility: Constructing Aristocracy in England and France 900-1300* (Harlow: Pearson).

Curta, F. (2009) 'The archaeology of service settlements in Eastern Europe', in P. Górecki and N. van Deusen (eds), *Central and Eastern Europe in the Middle Ages* (London and New York: I.B. Tauris), 30-41.

Darvill, T. (1988) 'Excavations on the site of the early Norman castle at Gloucester, 1983-84', *Medieval Archaeology* 32: 1-49.

Davison, B.K. (1967) 'The origins of the castle in England: the Institute's research project', *Archaeological Journal* 124: 202-11.

Davison, B.K. (1969) 'Early earthwork castles: a new model', *Château Gaillard* 3: 37-47.

De Boüard, M. (1973-4) 'De l'aula au donjon: les fouilles de la motte de la chapelle à Doué-la-Fontaine, Xe-XIe siècle', *Archéologie Médiévale* 3-4: 5-110.

De Jong, M. (2008) 'Charlemagne's balcony: the *solarium* in ninth-century narratives', in J.R. David and M. McCormick (eds), *The Long Morning of Medieval Europe: New Directions in Early Medieval Studies* (Aldershot: Ashgate), 277-89.

De Meulemeester, J. (1994) 'Le début du château: la motte castrale dans les Pays-Bas méridionaux', *Château Gaillard* 16: 121-30.

De Meulemeester, J. and O'Conor, K. (2007), 'Fortifications', in J. Graham-Campbell with M. Valor (eds), *The Archaeology of Medieval Europe*, vol. 1: *Eighth to Twelfth Centuries AD* (Aarhus: Aarhus University Press), 316-41.

Decaëns, J. and Dubois, A. (2009) *Le Château de Caen: Mille ans d'une forteresse dans la ville* (Caen: Publications du CRAHM).

Démians d'Archimbaud, G. (1981) *Les fouilles de Rougiers (Var): Contribution à l'archéologie de l'habitat rural médiéval en pays*

Bibliography

méditerranéen (Paris: Editions du Centre National de la Recherche Scientifique).

Diez, V., Allen, L., Riddler, I., Powell, A. and Bakels, C. (1998) *Mayenne, le Château*, vol. 5: *Etude de la céramique, des mobiliers isolés, de la faune et l'environment* (Nantes: SRA, Pays de la Loire).

Dormoy, C. (1997) 'L'expertise dendrochronologique du donjon de Loches (Indre-et-Loire): des donnés fondamentales pour sa datation', *Archéologie Médiévale* 27: 73-87.

Driscoll, S.T. (1998) 'Formalising the mechanisms of state power: early Scottish lordship from the ninth to the thirteenth centuries', in S. Foster, A. Macinnes and R. MacInnes (eds), *Scottish Power Centres: From the Early Middle Ages to the Twentieth Century* (Glasgow: Cruithne), 32-58.

Duby, G. (1977) *The Chivalrous Society* (London: University of California Press).

Eales, R. (1990) 'Royal power and castles in Norman England', *Medieval Knighthood* 3: 49-78.

Early, R. (1998) *Mayenne, le Château*, vol. 1: *Synthèse globale du Projet* (Nantes: SRA, Pays de la Loire).

Early, R. (2002) 'Château de Mayenne: les témoins archéologiques de l'evolution d'un centre de pouvoir entre le Xe et le XIIe siècle', *Château Gaillard* 20: 247-62.

Ekroll, Ø. (1998) 'Norwegian medieval castles: building on the edge of Europe', *Château Gaillard* 18: 65-74.

Ervynck, A. (1992) 'Medieval castles as top-predators of the feudal system: an archaeozoological approach', *Château Gaillard* 15: 151-59.

Ervynck, A. (2004) 'Orant, pugnant, laborant. The diet of the three orders within the feudal society of medieval Europe', in S.J. O'Day, W. van Neer and A. Ervynck (eds), *Behaviour Behind Bones* (Oxford: Oxbow), 215-23.

Ervynck, A. and Woollett, J. (2006) 'Top predator or survivor? The castle of Sugny as seen through its animal remains', in D. Sarlet (ed.), *Les cahiers de l'urbanisme: mélanges d'archéologie médiévale, liber amicorum en Hommage à André Matthys* (Liège: Mardaga), 78-89.

Ettel, P. (2008) 'Frühmittelalterliche Burgen in Deutschland – zum Stand der Forschung', *Château Gaillard* 23: 161-87.

Fehring, G.P. (1991) *The Archaeology of Medieval Germany: An Introduction* (London: Routledge).

Ferrand, G. (2006) 'Centre et habitat dispersé: le *Castrum* de Mouret (Aveyron) au milieu des champs', *Château Gaillard* 22: 129-37.

Fichtenau, H. (1991) *Living in the Tenth Century: Mentalities and Social Orders* (Chicago: University of Chicago Press).

Bibliography

Flambard Héricher, A-M. (2002) 'Fortifications de terre et residences en Normandie (XIe-XIIIe siècles)', *Château Gaillard* 20: 87-100.

Fossier, R. (1982) *Enfance de l'Europe*, 2 vols (Paris: Presses Universitaires de France).

Foucault, M. (1980) *Power/Knowledge: Selected Interviews and Other Writings 1972-1977*, ed. C. Gordon (Hassocks: Harvester).

Francovich, R. (2008) 'The beginnings of hilltop villages in Early Medieval Tuscany', in J.R. David and M. McCormick (eds), *The Long Morning of Medieval Europe: New Directions in Early Medieval Studies* (Ashgate: Aldershot), 55-82.

Francovich, R. and Hodges, R. (2003) *Villa to Village: The Transformation of the Roman Countryside* (London: Duckworth).

Friedrich, R. (1994) 'Die frühen Perioden der Motte Husterknupp. Neue Untersuchungen zur Keramik', *Château Gaillard*, 16: 207-13.

Friedrich, R. (2006) 'Die Burgenentwicklung im Rhein-Gebiet und ihr Bezug zum Altsiedelland', *Château Gaillard* 22: 149-61.

Glick, T.F. (1995) *From Muslim Fortress to Christian Castle: Social and Cultural Change in Medieval Spain* (Manchester and New York: Manchester University Press).

Glick, T.F. (2005) *Islamic and Christian Spain in the Early Middle Ages* (Leiden and Boston: Brill).

Goodall, J. (2011) *The English Castle, 1066-1650* (New Haven and London: Yale University Press).

Graham-Campbell, J. with Valor, M. (eds) (2007) *The Archaeology of Medieval Europe*, vol. 1: *Eighth to Twelfth Centuries AD* (Aarhus: Aarhus University Press).

Hansson, M. (2001) 'The minor "castles" of the gentry in Småland, Sweden', *Castelli Maris Baltici* 5: 67-74.

Hansson, M. (2006) *Aristocratic Landscape: The Spatial Ideology of the Medieval Aristocracy* (Lund: Lund Studies in Historical Archaeology).

Henning, J. (2005) 'Civilisation versus Barbarians? Fortification techniques and politics in the Carolingian and Ottonian borderlands', in F. Curta (ed.), *Borders, Barriers, and Ethnogenesis: Frontiers in Late Antiquity and the Middle Ages* (Turnhout: Brepols), 23-34.

Herrmann, J. (1966) *Tornow und Vorberg. Ein Beitrag zur Frühgeschichte der Lausitz* (Berlin: Akademie-Verlag).

Herrnbrodt, A. (1958) *Der Husterknupp, eine niederrheinische Burganlage des frühen Mittelalters* (Cologne: Bohlau).

Hicks, L.V. (2009) 'Magnificent entrances and undignified exits: chronicling the symbolism of castle space in Normandy', *Journal of Medieval History* 35: 52-69.

Higham, R. and Barker, P. (1992) *Timber Castles* (London: Batsford).

Higham, R. and Barker, P. (2000) *Hen Domen, Montgomery: A Timber*

Bibliography

Castle on the English-Welsh Border (Exeter: University of Exeter Press).

Hodges, R. (1988) 'Origins of the English castle', *Nature* 6169: 112-13.

Impey, E. (ed.) (2008) *The White Tower* (New Haven and London: Yale University Press).

Impey, E. and Lorans, E. (1998) 'Langeais, Indre-et-Loire. An archaeological and historical study of the early *donjon* and its environs', *Journal of the British Archaeological Association* 151: 43-106.

Janssen, H. (2008) 'Medieval castle research in the Netherlands', *Château Gaillard* 23: 237-51.

Jost, B. (2002) 'Muenzenberg (Hesse) and its relationship to later twelfth-century castles', in G. Meirion-Jones, E. Impey and M. Jones (eds), *The Seigneurial Residence in Western Europe AD c. 800-1600* (Oxford: Archaeopress), 179-87.

Kemethmüller, L. (2011) 'The history of the castle landscape in the German Spessart', *Concilium medii aevi* 14: 93-9.

Kristiansen, K. (2008) 'Do we need the "archaeology of Europe"?', *Archaeological Dialogues* 15.1: 5-25.

Kühtreiber, T. (1999) 'The medieval castle Lanzenkirchen in Lower Austria: reconstruction of economical and ecological development of an average-sized manor (12th-15th century)', *Archaeologia Polona* 37: 135-44.

Kupfer, M. (2011) 'The cult of images in light of pictorial graffiti at Doué-la-Fontaine', *Early Medieval Europe* 19.2: 125-52.

Laffont, P-Y. (2009) *Châteaux du Vivarais: Pouvoirs et peuplement en France méridionale. Du haut Moyen Âge au XIIIe siècle* (Rennes: Presses Universitaires de Rennes).

Le Goff, J. (2005) *The Birth of Europe* (Oxford: Blackwell).

Liebgott, N-K. and Olsen, R.A. (2008) 'Castellology in Scandinavia at the beginning of the 2nd millennium', *Château Gaillard* 23: 341-48.

Link, F. (2009) 'The internationalism of German castle research: Bodo Ebhardt, his European network, and the construction of "castle knowledge"', *Public Archaeology* 8.4, 325-50.

Lobbedey, U. (2003) 'Carolingian royal palaces: the state of research from an architectural historian's viewpoint', in C. Cubitt (ed.), *Court Culture in the Early Middle Ages. Proceedings of the First Alcuin Conference* (Turnhout: Brepols), 129-54.

Loveluck, C. (2005) 'Rural settlement hierarchy in the age of Charlemagne', in J. Story (ed.), *Charlemagne: Empire and Society* (Manchester: Manchester University Press), 230-58.

Manning, C. (2002) 'Low-level roofs in Irish great towers', *Château Gaillard* 20: 137-40.

Marshall, P. (2002a) 'The ceremonial function of the donjon in the twelfth century', *Château Gaillard* 20: 141-51.

Marshall, P. (2002b) 'The Great Tower as residence in the territories of the Norman and Angevin kings of England', in G. Meirion-Jones, E. Impey and M. Jones (eds), *The Seigneurial Residence in Western Europe AD c. 800-1600* (Oxford: Archaeopress), 27-44.

Matthys, A. (1991) 'Les fortifications du XIe siècle entre Lesse et Semois', in. H.W. Böhme (ed.), *Burgen der Salierzeit*, Teil 1: *In den Nordlichen Landschaften des Reiches* (Sigmaringen: Jan Thorbecke Verlag), 225-80.

McNeill, T.E. (2006) 'The view from the top', in D. Sarlet (ed.), *Les cahiers de l'urbanisme: mélanges d'archéologie médiévale, liber amicorum en Hommage à André Matthys* (Liège: Mardaga), 122-7.

Mesqui, J. (1991-3) *Châteaux et enceintes de la France médiévale*, 2 vols (Paris: Picard).

Meyer, W. (1994) 'Frühe Burgen im Lichte der schriftlichen Quellen und der archäologischen Befunde', *Château Gaillard* 16: 300-7.

Mignot, P., Dehon, D. and Henrotay, D. (2004) 'Le basse-cour du Château médiéval en Wallonie. État de la question archéologique', *Château Gaillard* 21: 229-41.

Mogren, M. (1996) 'Current Swedish castle research: the hinterland emphasis', *Castella Maris Baltici* 2: 111-16.

Mouton, D. (2008) *Mottes castrales en Provence: Les origines de la fortification privée au moyen âge* (Paris: Éditions de la Maison des Sciences de l'Homme).

O'Conor, K.D. (1998) *The Archaeology of Medieval Rural Settlement in Ireland* (Dublin: Royal Irish Academy).

O'Conor, K.D. (2002) 'Motte castles in Ireland: permanent fortresses, residences and manorial centres', *Château Gaillard* 20: 173-82.

O'Conor, K.D., Brady, N., Connon, A. and Fidalgo-Romo, C. (2010) 'The Rock of Lough Cé, Co. Roscommon', in T. Finan (ed.), *Medieval Lough Cé: History, Archaeology and Landscape* (Dublin: Four Courts Press), 15-40.

O'Keeffe, T. (2001) 'Concepts of "castle" and the construction of identity in medieval and post-medieval Ireland', *Irish Geography* 34.1: 69-88.

O'Keeffe, T. (2007) *Archaeology and the Pan-European Romanesque* (London: Duckworth).

Oram, R.D. (2006) 'Castles and colonists in twelfth- and thirteenth-century Scotland: the case of Moray', *Château Gaillard* 22: 289-98.

Oram, R.D. (2008) 'Royal and lordly residence in Scotland c. 1050 to c. 1250: an historiographical review and critical revision', *Antiquaries Journal* 88: 165-89.

Pluskowski, A. (2007) 'Communicating through skin and bone: appropriating animal bodies in medieval Western European seigneurial culture', in A. Pluskowski (ed.), *Breaking and Shaping Beastly Bodies: Animals as Material Culture in the Middle Ages* (Oxford: Oxbow), 32-51.

Bibliography

Purton, P. (2009) *A History of the Early Medieval Siege, c. 450-1200* (Woodbridge: Boydell).

Querrien, A. (2008) 'Les formes circulaires de l'espace bâti et agricole au Moyen Âge: tracé, mesure et partage', *Archéologie Médiévale* 38: 123-58.

Racinet, P. (2010) 'Dix ans de fouilles programmées à Boves (Somme): autour d'un château (début Xe-fin XIVe siècle)', in J. Chapelot (ed.), *Trente ans d'archéologie médiévale en France. Un bilan pour un avenir. IXe congrès international de la Société d'Archéologie Médiévale (Vincennes, 16-18 Juin 2006)* (Caen: Publications du CRAHM), 257-70.

Randsborg, K. (2003) 'Bastrup – Europe. A massive Danish donjon from 1100', *Acta Archaeologica* 74: 65-122.

Renn, D. (1994) 'Burhgeat and gonfanon: two sidelights from the Bayeux Tapestry', *Anglo-Norman Studies* 16: 177-98.

Renoux, A. (2010) 'Châteaux, palais et habitats aristocratiques fortifiés et semi-fortifiés', in J. Chapelot (ed.), *Trente ans d'archéologie médiévale en France. Un bilan pour un avenir. IXe congrès international de la Société d'Archéologie Médiévale (Vincennes, 16-18 Juin 2006)* (Caen: Publications du CRAHM), 239-56.

Reuter, T. (1997) 'The "feudal revolution"', *Past and Present* 155: 177-95.

Reynolds, S. (1994) *Fiefs and Vassals: The Medieval Evidence Reinterpreted* (Oxford: Oxford University Press).

Roberts, B.K. (2008) *Landscapes, Documents and Maps: Villages in Northern England and Beyond AD 900-1250* (Oxford: Oxbow).

Roland, A. 2003: 'Once more into the stirrups: Lynn White Jr., "Medieval Technology and Social Change"', *Technology and Culture*, 44.3: 574-85.

Samson, R. (1987) 'The Merovingian nobleman's home: castle or villa?', *Journal of Medieval History* 13: 287-315.

Saunders, A.D. (1977) 'Five castle excavations: reports on the Institute's research project into the origins of the castle in England', *Archaeological Journal* 134: 1-156.

Schut, P.A.C. (2003) *De Montferlandsche berg, het sieraad der tusschen IJssel en Rijn gelegene landen. De motte Montferland (gemeente Bergh) en een overzicht van motteversterkingen in Gelderland* (Amersfoort: Nederlandse Archeologische Rapporten).

Serjeantson, D. (2006) 'Birds: food and a mark of status', in C.M. Woolgar, D. Serjeantson and T. Waldron (eds), *Food in Medieval England: Diet and Nutrition* (Oxford: Oxford University Press), 131-47

Shapland, M. (2008) 'St Mary's, Broughton, Lincolnshire: a thegnly tower-nave in the late Anglo-Saxon Landscape', *Archaeological Journal* 165: 471-519.

Bibliography

Smith, S.V. (2009) 'Materializing resistant identities among the medieval peasantry: an examination of dress accessories from English rural settlement sites', *Journal of Material Culture* 14:3: 309-32.

Svensson, E. (2008) *The Medieval Household: Daily Life in Castles and Farmsteads* (Turnhout: Brepols).

Sykes, N. and Carden, R.F. (2011) 'Were Fallow Deer spotted (OE *pohha*/*pocca*) in Anglo-Saxon England? Reviewing the evidence for *Dama dama dama* in early medieval Europe', *Medieval Archaeology* 55: 139-62.

Thompson, M.W. (1991) *The Rise of the Castle* (Cambridge: Cambridge University Press).

Toubert, P (1973) *Les Structures du Latium médiéval: le Latium méridional et la Sabine du IXe siècle à la fin du XIIe siècle* (Rome: École Française de Rome).

Valenti, M. and Salvatori, F. (2008) 'Animal bones: synchronous and diachronic distribution as patterns of socially determined meat consumption in the early and high middle ages in central and northern Italy', in A. Pluskowski (ed.), *Breaking and Shaping Beastly Bodies: Animals as Material Culture in the Middle Ages* (Oxford: Oxbow), 170-88.

Van de Noort, R. (2011) *North Sea Archaeologies: A Maritime Biography, 10,000 BC-AD 1500*. Oxford: Oxford University Press.

Van Strydonck, M. and Vanthournout, C. (1996) 'Dating the "Hoge Andjoen" motte at Werken (prov. W. Fl.)', in M. Lodewijckx (ed.), *Archaeological and Historical Aspects of West-European Societies* (Leuven: Acta Archaeologica Lovaniensia Monographiae), 441-52.

Ward-Perkins, J.B. (1981) *Roman Imperial Architecture* (New York: Penguin).

Wheatley, A. (2008) 'The White Tower in medieval myth and legend', in E. Impey (ed.), *The White Tower* (New Haven and London: Yale University Press), 277-88.

White, L. (1962) *Medieval Technology and Social Change* (Oxford: Oxford University Press).

Wickham, C. (1981) *Early Medieval Italy: Central Power and Local Society 400-1000* (London: Macmillan).

Wickham, C. (1985) *Il Problema dell'incastellamento nell'Italia Centrale* (Florence: Edizioni All'insegna Del Giglio).

Wickham, C. (2001) 'Society', in R. McKitterick (ed.), *The Early Middle Ages: Europe 400-1000* (Oxford: Oxford University Press), 59-94.

Wickham, C. (2005) *Framing the Early Middle Ages: Europe and the Mediterranean, 400-800* (Oxford: Oxford University Press).

Williams, A. (1992) 'A bell-house and a burh-geat: lordly residences in England before the Norman Conquest', *Medieval Knighthood* 4: 221-40.

Bibliography

Williams, A. (2008) *The World before Domesday: The English Aristocracy 870-1066* (London: Continuum).

Zabiela, G. (1996) 'The end of wooden fortifications in Lithuania', *Castella Maris Baltici* 2: 223-8.

Zeune, J. (1996) *Burgen, Symbole der Macht: Ein neues Bild der mittelalterlichen Burg* (Regensberg: Verlag).

Index

Page numbers are in **bold** where they refer to an image.

Index

Index

Index